ENDORSEMENTS

There is a power God freely supplies that is available to all believers. It is a miraculous power that can move beyond the natural laws of physics and make the impossible a reality. At His ascension, Jesus said, "You shall receive power when the Holy Spirit has come upon you." The Holy Spirit releases this power in the lives of believers to defeat the works of the enemy.

In his new book, *Releasing the Miraculous,* Dr. James Tan explains the deep things of the Spirit in an easy-to-read and easy-to-understand way. Through his extensive years of study and through his own personal experience, Dr. Tan masterfully leads the reader into a deeper understanding of how the gifts of the Holy Spirit are administered. When the principles that he teaches are applied, victory is the result.

I have known Dr. James Tan both personally and through the work of his ministry. He is a true scholar of the Bible and a trusted teacher. He walks in wisdom well beyond his years, and I believe his character and his teaching to be flawless.

I am honored to endorse him and recommend his new book, *Releasing the Miraculous.*

Dr. Larry Ollison
Author, Pastor, and International Speaker

D1508560

The moment I met James I recognized he had been gifted by God with an apostolic anointing. Through his Facebook postings, I have come to know him as Just James. To some, Just James may not sound apostolic. However, an attitude of humility and transparency has created a conduit through which the divine nature of God can be made manifest to all. God gives grace to the humble and exalts them in due time. A teaching on the gifts of the Holy Spirit is so needed by the modern-day Church. What is even more needed is an author who has been touched by God's grace and understands the gifts. The gifts magnify the Giver. As I read the manuscript for this book, the teaching magnified the Giver of every good and perfect gift. The Church will be blessed, Christ will be manifested, and lives will be forever changed. It's my honor to endorse *Releasing the Miraculous: Walking in All Nine Gifts of the Holy Spirit.*

BILL ANNIS
Pastor and President, Faith Christian Fellowship
Canada

My family and I have been the beneficiaries of the power, the manifestations, and the supernatural miracles of the Holy Spirit. James Tan has so eloquently taught, explained, and encouraged that we covet and profit from God's all purposeful gifts. I cannot conceive of being without God's supernatural Spirit within me. Glean everything you can from this writing.

DR. DEAN RADTKE
CEO and Founder of The Institute of
Ministry Management and Leadership

This book contains a simple, yet profound, explanation of the nine gifts and manifestations of the power of the Holy Spirit, the third person of the Godhead. It is full of information and revelation that the reader will both enjoy and appreciate.

I met Dr. James Tan when he attended one of my Helping Inspire Ministries conferences. As I was leading the meeting, I could sense this young man's spirit was holding a lot of knowledge. I called him forward and told him, "I know you have something to share, even though I don't know you. But thank you for holding what you have out of respect since this was not your meeting."

Soon, I released Dr. Tan to share what the Lord had given him. He didn't unload his complete revelation all at once, but he was careful to speak an exhortation to us by the unction of the Holy Spirit. This took our service to another level.

Dr. Tan is a great blessing to me and to those in our ministry. I know his teaching in *Releasing the Miraculous: Walking in All Nine Gifts of the Holy Spirit* will bless you as well!

Dr. Elizabeth Pruitt-Sloan
President, Helping Inspire Ministries

In a day when there's much confusion about the manifestation of the Holy Spirit gifts, and even some denial of their existence, Dr. Tan has done a wonderful job of not only defining the operation of the gifts but also given a biblical and practical use of them. After reading Dr. Tan's book on the manifestation of the Holy Spirit, it will help enable every believer to be used of God in a greater measure and bring blessings to the church as well has the world.

JIM H. ANDREWS

Rhema, Peru

Dr. James has the ability of taking a subject that could otherwise seem overwhelming and difficult to understand and making it seem like you just walked into a room and turned on the light.

That's what he has done with his book on the gifts of the Spirit. As only he can do, he divides the Word so effortlessly. The way he explains the operation of the gifts and how they flow into one another seamlessly, and how it is that way with the things of God in the scripture, really brings illumination.

He is a gifted teacher who makes the Word come alive. He also has that rare gift in his writing that when you read it you can almost hear him saying it.

Dr. James is such a gifted teacher of the Word and also a gifted writer. You will see as you read things will begin to open up and illumination will come—and the light will come on!

RAYGENE WILSON

Pastor, West Coast Life Church

Murrieta, CA

Dr. James Tan's *Releasing the Miraculous* recognizes the importance of God's Word activated by faith but also the imperative and often overlooked person of the Holy Spirit operating through us by His gifts. This is a key book to have in your library. It is highly recommended reading and studying so you can experience a mighty *release* of the *miraculous* in *your* life and ministry.

DR. STEVE ANDERSON
President, Transworld Accrediting
Commission International

In this book, James Tan expresses his deep desire to enable every reader to identify the spiritual equipment that the Father has granted him through the ministry of the Holy Spirit.

Each page of *Releasing the Miraculous* is filled with a clear teaching about the gifts of the Spirit. The depth of the doctrinal research gives the reader a sound understanding of each gift.

But, as our brother James of the Bible, James Tan is very pragmatic in his walk with God—the doctrine must be applicable to the believer in his everyday life and in the local church. Therefore, the author has made a point to show the practical side of the operations of the gifts. Through the many personal examples, you will learn how to trust and to cooperate with the Holy Spirit *today*. No doubt, James knows what he is teaching about! This book counts among the *must read!*

MARIE-HÉLÈNE MOULIN
Pastor of Ekklesia 21
Nice, France

RELEASING THE MIRACULOUS

RELEASING THE MIRACULOUS

WALKING IN ALL NINE GIFTS
OF THE HOLY SPIRIT

JAMES TAN

Published by Harrison House Publishers
Shippensburg, PA 17257

Cover design by Eileen Rockwell
Interior design Terry Clifton

ISBN 13 TP: 978-1-6803-1584-4
ISBN 13 eBook: 978-1-6803-1585-1
ISBN 13 HC: 978-1-6803-1587-5
ISBN 13 LP: 978-1-6803-1586-8

For Worldwide Distribution, Printed in the U.S.A.
1 2 3 4 5 6 7 8 / 25 24 23 22 21

For Bon and Boots

ACKNOWLEDGMENT

Thank you to Pastor Ginger Hogg Terry of Faith Triumphant Church, Portales, New Mexico, for helping with the editing of the original draft.

CONTENTS

Foreword by *Dr. Pat Harrison* 1

Foreword by *Lynne Hammond* 3

Introduction 5

CHAPTER ONE   The Word of Wisdom 35

CHAPTER TWO   The Word of Knowledge 57

CHAPTER THREE   Faith 81

CHAPTER FOUR   Healings 105

CHAPTER FIVE   The Working of Miracles 131

CHAPTER SIX   Prophecy 153

CHAPTER SEVEN   Discerning of Spirits 175

CHAPTER EIGHT   Tongues and Interpretation of Tongues . . .197

CHAPTER NINE   The River of the Spirit 221

FOREWORD

James Tan is a gifted and anointed man of God. His simple but profound teachings bring you into great revelation and understanding.

He is a scholar of the Word of God. His education along with his calling and anointing bring you to the edge of your seat when hearing him minister and watching him flow in the Spirit.

This book, *Releasing the Miraculous: Walking in All Nine Gifts of the Holy Spirit,* will not only bring revelation to you but a strong desire to know the Holy Spirit and how He flows.

While reading this book, get ready to rejoice, shout, and meditate on the Word.

Dr. Pat Harrison
Cofounder and President of
Faith Christian Fellowship International

FOREWORD

What you hold in your hand is much like a treasure chest. Pay close attention, because as your fingers turn from page to page there are hidden facets of heaven for your heart to discover, embrace, and experience.

James Tan is one whom I would like to call a heavenly lexicon. Lexicons tend to carry the language and vocabulary of a person or a place and translate it for easy mental digestion. And James forms words around the spiritual atmosphere many times we feel but cannot name—like a verbal bridge between heaven to earth.

Many can feel it; James verbalizes it.

I first met James when he was a student at Rhema Bible Training Center in Singapore. I knew from the moment I met him that God had a wild path laid out ahead for him. He was quick and obedient to jump into the call.

The words that come out of James act much like a door for me. As he verbally maneuvers through the landscape of the text, it's as if he is turning a doorknob and allowing my spirit to enter into uncharted territory, like rooms of undiscovered revelation. The depth that he stewards has been supernaturally placed within him for such a time as this.

There is no doubt in my mind the Church is heading into some of its greatest days. While the days ahead hold extraordinary beauty for us to behold, they also hold circumstances that will inevitably call us to rise up in our most holy of faiths—causing us to lean full force into the divinely established tools that James so eloquently lays out in this book.

These tools are not just for us to pick up and collect only as knowledge. They were created for us to embrace, digest, and utilize at full capacity in the very depths of our beings.

My prayer for your heart is that you would graciously embrace the gifts that have been strategically created by heaven. That the depths of your being would grab hold of them to the very fullest. And that you would know without a shadow of a doubt that you, my darling and daring saint, have been called to the Kingdom for such a time as this.

The time has come.

You are deeply loved,
LYNNE HAMMOND

INTRODUCTION

I was brought up in a very nominal Catholic family. Signs, wonders, the miraculous, and biblical spirituality were not part of my upbringing. Shortly after I became born again in my early teens, I was invited to attend my first Spirit-filled, charismatic church service.

Stepping into the sanctuary that Sunday morning, I did not know what to make of the service. I saw people clapping or with their hands lifted. There was repetitive singing of choruses with some people, including the worship leader, even crying. It was all so foreign to me—plus I didn't quite know what to do with my hands. They all seemed to alternate between enthusiastically repeating choruses and singing in this unusual sounding, but strangely soothing, unknown language. Then, just when I thought it couldn't possibly get any weirder, the service quietened down, and the room fell silent.

After what seemed like the longest silence I had ever experienced in church, someone toward the front of the hall spoke loudly and authoritatively in that unrecognizable language I had heard them all singing.

Without missing a beat, as soon as he stopped speaking, one of the leaders in the front of the hall walked up to a microphone and announced, "I have the interpretation to that tongue. Hear what the Holy Spirit is saying...."

I don't remember all that followed, but I do remember that as he started interpreting those bizarre words into English, I was suddenly aware of a peaceful yet majestic presence in the room. The interpretive message didn't last long, but as he continued delivering, I started tearing up as the presence I sensed seemed to settle on me. I instinctively knew that something divine was speaking to us. For the rest of the service, even as we went through the preliminaries and then the closing of the service, I continued to sense that presence on me. I knew I had met God at a level that my mind could not comprehend. This thought lingered in me: *God still speaks!*

A CONTINUAL FLOW

The manifestation of the Holy Spirit is a subject that has always caused controversy, both in and outside the Church. Perhaps it always will, but it should be considered of great importance to any believer. Manifestations speak to the continuity of the Holy Spirit's ministry.

The Holy Spirit dwelling in us seeks to express the Kingdom of God through us. He does this by the workings commonly called *spiritual gifts*. An understanding of the clear scriptural definitions of His workings through the nine manifestations listed in First Corinthians 12, gives us room to have expectation and the daring to give expression to His operations.

The Holy Spirit dwelling in us seeks to express the Kingdom of God through us. He does this by the workings commonly called *spiritual gifts*.

Even a casual reading of either the Old or New Testaments will leave one with the distinct impression that those who had a relationship with God walked in the supernatural. The supernatural was not only required to have a relationship with God, but because of their relationship, the prophets lived in a unique flow of the miraculous. This was not just true in their personal lives; it is clear that the corporate meetings portrayed in the New Testament had an expectation of the supernatural as well.

While this miraculous lifestyle was primarily confined to the kings, prophets, and priests in the Old Testament, the New Testament saw a dramatic shift. The miraculous was made available to all believers.

> *"And these signs will follow those who believe: In My name they will cast out demons; they will speak with new tongues; they will take up serpents; and if they drink anything deadly, it will by no means hurt them; they will lay hands on the sick, and they will recover.' So then, after the Lord had spoken to them, He was received up into heaven, and sat down at the right hand of God. And they went out and preached everywhere, the Lord working with them and confirming the word through accompanying signs. Amen."*
> MARK 16:17-18,20

The purpose of this supernatural endowment on all believers was primarily for the proclamation and establishment of the gospel. The method by which God chose this proclamation was so that "everyday believers" could be made witnesses of the Living God. The supernatural was part of the discipleship process. Why would a supernatural God build a supernatural organism—the Church—in a natural way?

> *"But you shall receive power when the Holy Spirit has come upon you; and you shall be witnesses to Me in Jerusalem, and in all Judea and Samaria, and to the end of the earth."*
>
> ACTS 1:8

Too many people have misunderstood that verse to mean that they need to be involved in some form of evangelism or witnessing. God's intention was not just that we "do" witnessing but that we become witnesses. A supernatural message requires supernatural witnesses.

God's intention was not just that we "do" witnessing, but that we become witnesses.

The key to this outpouring of the supernatural in and through believers was that they had *all* received the gift of the Holy Spirit as promised by Jesus and then by Peter at Pentecost.

This experience with the Holy Spirit brought the believers past intellectual assent to a creed of beliefs and into an actual relationship with the Spirit of God Himself. As it has been noted, it is one thing to know the Bible, but it is another to know the Author. These early believers not only acknowledged God's work in their personal regeneration and sanctification, they also knew Him well enough to recognize His movements. They knew when He came, where He came, and even how He came!

The Apostle Paul was such an advocate of an encounter with the Holy Spirit that he unashamedly asked professing believers if they had taken the further step of receiving the Holy Spirit (Acts 19:2). The result was a repeat of the upper room Pentecost experience; the Ephesians had their own encounter with the Holy Spirit.

> *"And when Paul had laid his hands upon them, the Holy Ghost came on them; and they spoke with tongues and prophesied."*
>
> ACTS 19:6

Every believer who is open to the fullness of the Spirit has great possibilities and unlimited power within them. This is not just because of the Spirit's indwelling but also because the potential of the Spirit's outpouring.

> *"And they were all filled with the Holy Ghost, and began to speak with other tongues, as the Spirit gave them utterance."*
>
> ACTS 2:4

Every believer who is open to the fullness of the Spirit has great possibilities and unlimited power within.

This single verse forever changed the spiritual landscape. It opened supernatural possibilities to more than a select few. The immediate sign of the indwelling of the Holy Spirit was that all who were in the upper room spoke in tongues.

As the apostle James would later say:

> *"Behold also the ships, which though they be so great, and are driven of fierce winds, yet are they turned about with a very small helm, whithersoever the governor listeth. Even so the tongue is a little member, and boasteth great things. Behold, how great a matter a little fire kindleth!"*
>
> *"But the tongue can no man tame; it is an unruly evil, full of deadly poison."*
>
> JAMES 3:4-5,8 (KJV)

The tongue is not just a rudder that steers the ship, but it can also be an unruly evil that cannot be tamed by man. This is undoubtedly why the first instrument of man that the Holy Spirit took over was the tongue. God was doing what man could not in taming the tongue. And in doing so, the Holy Spirit was taking control of the rudder of man's life and pointing it in the direction of the supernatural. Praying in tongues opens you, a believer, up to the flow of the Spirit in a way that nothing else can.

PAUL THE PROTOTYPE!

Paul was such a prototype. He was not a disciple while Jesus was about His earthly ministry. He had no access to the private conversations that Peter, James, and John had with Jesus. All of Paul's interaction with the risen Lord was in the spiritual realm, and yet, he received enough insight and enlightenment on the finished work of Calvary that God appointed him to write a major part of the New Testament. He knew Jesus so intimately that even Peter, who was in the inner circle, confessed that some of Paul's revolutionary writings were beyond him (2 Pet. 3:15-16).

Undoubtedly, praying in tongues was one of Paul's major keys to receiving the rich revelation that he did. He stated in First Corinthians 14:18 that, "I thank my God I speak with tongues more than you all...."

A continual flow of tongues is the doorway to a continual flow of the supernatural!

A continual flow of tongues is the doorway to a continual flow of the supernatural!

Speaking in tongues was new and exciting when I first discovered it. I was baptized in the Holy Ghost two months after I became born again. There was many a night where I would go into the early morning praying in the Spirit. One time I had a distinct experience in the Spirit where I felt and saw my physical body from the vantage point of my spirit. From that vantage point, I saw that my body wasn't who I really was. I was a spirit being.

As it has been said, each of us is a spirit, we have a soul, and we live in body. This encounter marked my life. All my studies and current ministry spring from an understanding of the division of the spirit man from the soul and body. One of the benefits of praying in tongues is that our spirit man is sensitized above our soul and physical man. This, in turn, causes our spirits to be more aware of spiritual things. And being spiritually sensitive is the key to all things supernatural.

A MESSAGE ABOUT MANIFESTATIONS

Opening the definitive chapter on spiritual manifestations in First Corinthians, Paul commands: "Now concerning spiritual gifts, brethren, I would not have you ignorant" (1 Cor. 12:1 KJV).

The Corinthians' ignorance was not because of a lack of manifestations in their midst. Indeed, they "come behind in no gift" (1 Cor. 1:7 KJV). Instead, their ignorance was their failure to see the need for unity in the diversity of manifestations and that love was to be the unifying factor. The Corinthians' ignorance was due to a downgrading sense of commonality—familiarity with the gifts to the extent that they no longer considered them holy or sacred.

In many parts of the Body of Christ today, this verse would have to be interpreted differently. Rather than ignorance of the awesomeness of the manifestations, many today are simply ignorant of the gifts because of a lack of exposure.

Known as the "Prince of Preachers" in his day, it was said of the famed nineteenth-century preacher, Charles Haddon Spurgeon, that he was a kindly and generous man who was drawn to the poor. His ministry maintained outreach homes to shelter and feed the poor, and he would personally make pastoral visits to some of them.

One old lady he visited had bundled all her meager belongings together with her when she came to live in one of Spurgeon's ministry homes. The bundle mainly consisted of sentimental mementos that had no real significance to anyone else. On one such visit, Spurgeon politely walked around the room inspecting these items. He chanced upon a framed piece of paper that had some lines written on it. Enquiring about it, the old lady proudly informed him that it had been given to her by an old man that she had worked for. He was wealthy and she had been his personal caregiver for many years. As he lay dying, he asked her, "What can I do to show my appreciation for all you've done for me?"

When she did not respond, he proceeded to give her this piece of paper. After he passed away, she framed the letter as a souvenir of her time working for him.

Spurgeon asked to borrow the framed piece of paper promising to return it soon. He took it to the bank to have it verified and was informed that it was a valid check that hadn't been cashed!

Charles brought the check back to the illiterate old lady and informed her that if she would cash it, she would not be as impoverished as she appeared. She had not been in want for lack of finances but for lack of knowledge of what belonged to her.

Ignorance robs many believers of what is rightly theirs from the Father.

Since these gifts are meant to bring profit to all (1 Cor. 12:7), the absence of these gifts would then mean the opposite. We are in lack when the gifts are not in operation.

We are in lack when the gifts are not in operation.

The phrase, *"manifestation of the Spirit,"* that Paul used in First Corinthians 12:7 comes from *phanerosis*—the *Greek* word literally meaning "to shine forth." One of the purposes of the infilling of the Holy Spirit in the life of a believer is so that the light of God might shine through him or her the same way that the flow of electricity is expressed differently through the many appliances we have around us.

Earlier in the same chapter, Paul had clarified:

> *"Now there are diversities of gifts, but the same Spirit.*
> *And there are differences of administrations, but the*
> *same Lord. And there are diversities of operations, but*
> *it is the same God which worketh all in all."*
> 1 CORINTHIANS 12:4-6 (KJV)

This was a clear indication that there would be no need for limitation or imitation to the manifestations of the Spirit, but there would be specific and individualized inspiration for each believer. As believers, we find our place in the Body through the manifestations of the Spirit.

If nothing else, these two observations alone—the Holy Spirit wants to manifest through us and He wants us to find our place in the Body—should be enough to convince anyone that the gifts of the Spirit are for us today.

BUT ARE THEY FOR TODAY?

I occasionally encounter people with the attitude that the manifestations of the Spirit are not for this day but were just part of the history of the Church. To come to that position of Cessationism is usually caused by a pre-determined interpretation of Scripture used to defend this position. There is no scriptural support that signs, wonders, and manifestations of the Spirit ended with the early disciples. There is no historical support for that position, either. You cannot logically support that belief. Why would the great and glorious God we hear about in the Old and New Testaments suddenly chose to end this age in absolute silence and noninvolvement?

It does say in First Corinthians 13:8 that "Charity never faileth: but whether there be prophecies, they shall fail; whether there be tongues, they shall cease; whether there be knowledge, it shall vanish away" (KJV). But it must be asked, why do those who use this verse to purport the ending of the manifestations of the Spirit stop with tongues and prophecy?

Why not carry that interpretation to the rest of the verse and say that knowledge has also passed away?

"But when that which is perfect is come, then that which is in part shall be done away."
1 CORINTHIANS 13:10

This Scripture clarifies a simple point: there will be a future event when we see this perfection "face to face" (1 Cor. 13:12). This proves that manifestations of the Spirit are to continue in our day since we have not been face to face with that which is perfect.

I have also heard it argued that the "perfect" spoken of in verse 10 is the Bible, and since we now have all the canon of Scripture complete, we no longer need spiritual gifts. While it is definitely true that the Bible is complete, meaning that no other tongue, interpretation, prophecy, or vision will add to it, the Bible cannot be the *perfect* referred to in verse 10. To be clear, God's Word—all sixty-six books—is whole, complete, infallible, and the foundation of our faith, but the fact is that any Bible that we have access to is translated by man, no matter how qualified. Further, the many wonderful translations and paraphrases we have, however needful, should also be a clue that the Bible, as we have it, in and of itself is not perfect. Why would we need so many versions if it was "perfect"?

This is a complete misunderstanding of the role of spiritual gifts. The New Testament clearly dislodges the concept that spiritual gifts can add to the Scriptures. What we do see is that the early church would compare and corroborate any prophetic utterance or experience they had with the Old Testament scripture. They never used a vision or prophecy from their own pool of ministers to establish a doctrine or settle a dispute. Rather, we see that the "prophecy of Scripture" (2 Pet. 1:20) was always given deference over any light that came as a result of the spiritual gifts in manifestation.

Spiritual gifts do not add to the canon of Scripture, but they many times pinpoint and demonstrate Scripture.

Historically, not every believer has demonstrated the flow of the Spirit through his or her life, but it would be a grave error to judge what God is willing to do by what people have done. It would be an even greater error to say that God withdrew the manifestations because believers lost them through neglect.

The early Church fathers, direct disciples of the original disciples, Irenaeus, Tertullian, Chrysostom, and Augustine all made mention of the miraculous in their ministries.

The Waldenses in the twelfth century, the pioneering Quakers from the mid-seventeenth century, and early Methodists in the eighteenth century are some among entire early groups that also wrote of spiritual gifts in operation.

Spiritual manifestations never went away because the giver of those gifts, the Holy Spirit, never went away!

You could rightfully say that spiritual manifestations never went away because the giver of those gifts, the Holy Spirit, never went away!

IN EVERY AREA

Both at the personal level and in corporate gatherings, the gifts of the Spirit bring a supernatural element that causes all to see that God does indeed confound the wise with the foolish and despised (1 Cor. 12:27-29). This continually takes us out of the driver's seat, allowing us to ride shotgun. Spiritual gifts make it obvious that outside of our best capacities—intellectual or academic—the Lord can and does move supernaturally. The operations of the Spirit are meant to bless the vessel that they flow through—those within the household of faith that received from the manifestations and those yet to be believers.

The church in Acts was equipped to bring forth light and turn the world right side up, using the gifts of words of wisdom and knowledge to minister to people who would otherwise reject the gospel of Jesus as foolishness.

The church in Acts combated manifestations of the many heathen philosophies with the gift of healing and the working of miracles. The church in Acts was strengthened and endured fierce opposition from its many enemies with the gift of faith and the discerning of spirits.

The church in Acts was kept in a place of continual encouragement and edification through the vocal gifts of prophecy, tongues, and the interpretation of tongues.

All nine manifestations of the Spirit ensure that on a regular basis, in the midst of the believers, their testimony as well as those of the visiting skeptics would be "...the secrets of his heart made manifest; and so falling down on his face he will worship God, and report that God is in you of a truth" (1 Cor. 14:25 KJV).

> *"Of judgment, because the prince of this world is judged."*
>
> JOHN 16:11 (KJV)

One of the reasons for the Holy Spirit being sent to earth is for the purpose of executing judgment against the enemy. The way He does this is firstly through dwelling in believers and then by endowing those same believers with His power. The Holy Spirit seeks to express His divine self through the believers He dwells in. The perfect example of such an arrangement is Jesus Christ Himself.

Looking through the Gospels, we can see that Jesus performed no miracles and cast out no demons until He had an encounter with the Holy Spirit after His baptism in the Jordan. It was only after seeing the Spirit in the form of a descending dove that Jesus exercised authority over the devil in the wilderness, and then publicly declared that the anointing rested on Him.

> *"The Spirit of the Lord is upon me, because he hath anointed me to preach the gospel to the poor; he hath sent me to heal the brokenhearted, to preach deliverance to the captives, and recovering of sight to the*

blind, to set at liberty them that are bruised, To preach the acceptable year of the Lord."
LUKE 4:18-19 (KJV)

Jesus was fully God, and in coming to earth, was also fully man. The miracles Jesus demonstrated during His three and a half years of ministry were not done as God but as a man anointed with the Holy Spirit. He did this because He was our example.

"How God anointed Jesus of Nazareth with the Holy Spirit and with power, who went about doing good and healing all who were oppressed by the devil, for God was with Him."
ACTS 10:38

If He had performed the miracles as God, then that would have given us no path to follow after Him since none of us would qualify. But since He manifested miracles as a man anointed by God, we can all qualify!

Jesus operated under the same anointing, through the same Spirit, and in the same gifts that are promised to us.

As we will see in later chapters, every miracle and supernatural encounter that Jesus manifested was actually one or more of the nine gifts of the Spirit functioning through Him.

Jesus operated under the same anointing, through the same Spirit, and in the same gifts that are promised to us.

> *"...For this purpose the Son of God was manifested, that He might destroy the works of the devil."*
>
> 1 JOHN 3:8

These gifts are a direct assault on the kingdom of darkness because they are a direct expression of the life of God. They are literally weapons from heaven that cause otherwise ordinary men and women to become conduits of the life and power of God.

Another way to look at the gifts of the Spirit would be to see them as tools from heaven to establish God's plans on the earth. Why would God send you forth as His witness to proclaim His message but not equip you with what you need? As we have already seen, a supernatural message needs supernatural messengers, and supernatural messengers need supernatural equipment: the gifts of the Spirit. Since the proclamation and demonstration of the gospel was never intended to be restricted to just a select few, we can rightly conclude that the same heavenly equipment is also made available to all believers.

> *"And there appeared unto them cloven tongues like as of fire, and it sat upon each of them."*
>
> ACTS 2:3 (KJV)

When the Holy Spirit fell on the day of Pentecost, He did not just fill the obvious leaders; He sat on everyone in the room. There is a tongue of fire for each one of us! Just as Jesus is our personal Savior, the Holy Spirit is each believer's individual power source.

A GIFT-GIVING FAMILY

In Romans 12:6-8, we see that the Father gave the Church seven gifts:

> *"Having then gifts differing according to the grace that is given to us, let us use them: if prophecy, let us prophesy in proportion to our faith; or ministry, let us use it in our ministering; he who teaches, in teaching; he who exhorts, in exhortation; he who gives, with liberality; he who leads, with diligence; he who shows mercy, with cheerfulness."*

In Ephesians 4:11, we see Jesus giving the Church five gifts:

> *"And he gave some, apostles; and some, prophets; and some, evangelists; and some, pastors and teachers."* (KJV)

In First Corinthians 12:8-10, we see the Spirit giving the Church nine gifts:

> *"For to one is given the word of wisdom through the Spirit, to another the word of knowledge through the same Spirit, to another faith by the same Spirit, to another gifts of healings by the same Spirit, to another the working of miracles, to another prophecy, to another discerning of spirits, to another different kinds of tongues, to another the interpretation of tongues."*

As believers, we belong to a gift-giving family!

The gifts of the Father mentioned in Romans 12 are primarily for the strengthening of the local church.

The gifts of Jesus mentioned in Ephesians are for the local church, the Body of Christ at large, and the world in general.

The gifts of the Spirit mentioned in First Corinthians 12 are for both the local church and the world.

The gifts in these three passages make up the earthly life and ministry of Jesus.

While we are not all gifted with each and every one of the gifts, we do collectively have access to all of them. For example, not everyone is an apostle, but we are all apostolic to some extent. We may not all be gifted in mercy, but we can all be merciful.

As believers, we have the Holy Spirit living on the inside of us; we are co-seated with Christ in heavenly places and we have God as our Father! Why would we not have access to all these divine gifts and characteristics?

Individually, we have parts of these gifts. Collectively, as the Body of Christ, we have them all. Though we are not all as strong in some giftings as other people, that does not mean we do not have that gift in the form of a seed inside of us.

Which of these gifts is best? They all bring benefits; no part of the Godhead would ever give us something bad for us, nor is the Godhead in competition with itself, competing to see who gives the Church the best gifts. Every gift given is necessary and adds to us.

Like most people, I enjoy receiving gifts—not always because I want something but because receiving a gift is a sign someone is thinking of me and wants to let me know it. Giving gifts is a sign of love. I was totally intrigued after I became saved to hear that there were *spiritual gifts.*

It never occurred to me that God prepared gifts for us outside of the baby Jesus (remember, I grew up Catholic), but as soon as I did, the idea captivated me. I remember attending a class in church that was on the gifts, and as soon as I had an opportunity, I asked the minister teaching the class, "How can I know what my gifts are?"

I had been saved for under a year at that point and wasn't even out of high school, but I was hungry. I later found that the class was meant to be more theoretical than experiential. I suppose my question shocked the minister. He looked at me solemnly and said, "You need to grow more spiritually, read your Bible, and pray more before He will give you any gifts."

I was crushed. My joyful expectation of a gift from God had turned into something that I had to earn by "growing." To be sure, we all need to grow, and as we grow, our use of the gifts sharpens. Yet, the gifts are not a result of our maturity but a product of our Father's generosity.

The church in Corinth is proof of this. It was a church that had an overflow of all the gifts in operation, yet they were also the most divisive and carnal people that Paul wrote to in the New Testament.

These were just some of the problems Paul addressed in his epistle: the fractions they had (1 Cor. 1:12), immaturity (1 Cor. 3:3), condoning of sexual immorality (1 Cor. 5:1), their public legal disputes with other believers (1 Cor. 6:5-7), and the disrespect expressed for the Lord's table (1 Cor. 11:17). Clearly, if maturity were a necessity to receive the gifts, the Corinthian church would have had none of them.

We must not confuse receiving the gifts with our stewardship of them. The former is an act of grace; the latter is an act of appreciation and care.

Any gift received, natural or spiritual, can be used, abused, or ignored. Just as the Corinthians were abusing their gifts, Timothy was encouraged by Paul to stir up the gift in him (2 Tim. 1:6) that he clearly was ignoring.

The Greek word in First Corinthians 1. for "gifts" is *charisma*. This word comes from the basic noun, *charis* and is normally translated as *grace*. Grace is what is freely given that could not be earned. This means that the spiritual gifts are literally "grace gifts." They are not earned wages; they are grace gifts!

Maturity is obviously required in the skillful use of the gifts, but maturity is a lifelong pursuit. If God waited God waited until we were "mature" before flowing through us, perhaps none of us would ever be of any service to Him.

Actually, the method that I have observed the Lord using to mature us is that of "growing as we are going."

Actually, the method that I have observed the Lord using to mature us is that of "growing as we are going." In other words, we grow, not by hiding away until we grow up but by utilizing what we have in front of us. We see this principle in Hebrews 5:14:

> *"But strong meat belongeth to them that are of full age, even those who by reason of use have their senses exercised to discern both good and evil"* (KJV).

The Word and the Spirit have a way of speaking to us at whatever level we are at.

Once, in prayer, I had the Lord tell me plainly through tongues and interpretation, "The gifts are given." This word exploded on the inside of me. These manifestations are not something that God has yet to give us. They are called gifts because they have *already* been given to us; otherwise, how could they be called gifts?

THE ALL-ENCOMPASSING SPIRIT

This look at the gifts of the Spirit is really a look at aspects of the person of the Holy Spirit. As a member of the Godhead, He has every divine characteristic. He is *omniscient*—meaning all knowing. He is *omnipotent*—having all power. He is *omnipresent*—being everywhere at once. The manifestations of the Spirit are each a form of His divinity. Each gift in operation is like the spoke of a wheel.

Nothing about these gifts is natural except that they flow through natural men. Jesus summed up our encounter with the Holy Spirit simply:

"But you shall receive power when the Holy Spirit has come upon you; and you shall be witnesses to Me in Jerusalem, and in all Judea and Samaria, and to the end of the earth."

ACTS 1:8

Since Jesus instructed us to await a power encounter, we can then rightly say that all aspects of the Holy Spirit's interaction with us are in the realm of supernatural, divine power. That is why a relationship and a working understanding of the Holy Spirit and His gifts are not really an elective in our spiritual walk. We are literally powerless without them.

These gifts are so important from a divine perspective that all three members of the Godhead are involved in their operation on the earth.

*"Now there are diversities of gifts, but the same **Spirit**. And there are differences of administrations, but the same **Lord**. And there are diversities of operations, but it is the same **God** which worketh all in all."*

1 CORINTHIANS 12:4-6 (KJV)

Obviously, the Trinity is involved in all aspects of our salvation and walk as believers, but in the case of the gifts, God saw fit to specifically highlight in Scripture their corporate involvement.

GIFTS AND GROWTH

should read: There nine manifestations of the Spirit are in no way natural abilities, but it is equally important to know they are not a result of our growth in the things of God. These are gifts, and they are given without merit on our part. Indeed, if they were given because of our merit, they would be rewards, not gifts. Obviously, there is a side to how these gifts will manifest in our lives as we grow in the things of God but that would simply be how we handle the gifts that were *already given.*

Remember when you just got your driver's license? Now imagine the moment you passed your test that you were given a brand-new sports car. Would you drive and handle that sports car with a greater measure of skill and care if you had been driving for ten years? We can all grow in our handling and delivery of the spiritual gifts, but the gifts are not a result of our walk with Him. They are given as a result of His grace and goodness.

I remember having to pick up my sons at school before they got their driver's licenses. There were other older kids who were driving themselves, so I was always extra careful when I went to get my boys. Although those high schoolers knew how to drive, their skill and road manners were not always the greatest. You would expect that as they grew and logged more road hours, their skill would increase. So it is with us and the gifts that God has given us.

If God waited until we were all mature before He gave us anything, none of us would qualify. The way we get skilled in anything is by hands-on training. There will be opportunities and occasions where mistakes happen, but that's where leaders and the grace and mercy of God come in to help us.

The church in Corinth is a perfect example of the gifts in manifestation through imperfect and immature people. They had divisions of every kind. They had sexual immorality in their midst. They had abuse of the spiritual gifts in manifestation. It even appears that they might have had evil spirits in operation who called out "Jesus is cursed" in their gatherings. But despite all of that, Paul did not write telling them to cease allowing manifestations in their times together; rather, he wrote to instruct them on the proper use of the manifestations.

We do have a responsibility to grow and nurture our stewardship of the gifts, but again, that is only with the understanding that the gifts *were given in the first place* so that we would have something to steward.

Not only are these gifts not our natural abilities, they are also not a byproduct of our spiritual growth. Some have mistakenly thought that the wisdom Solomon received (1 Kings 3) was the word of wisdom. But that was wisdom that we can all move into as a result of growth. *There is a difference between manifestations of gifts and manifestations of growth!* And we need them both. Wisdom can grow in us by simply asking God for it (James 1:5), by heeding the Word of God, and through prayer (Eph. 1:17).

There is a difference between manifestations of gifts and manifestations of growth!

It is definitely within the functions of the unrenewed human mind to try to either explain away the supernatural or relegate it to the realm of superstition. These manifestations of the Spirit must be *neither* natural nor superstition because they flow from the Holy Spirit Himself. There must be a clear distinction between the gifts of the Holy Spirit and the growth of the human spirit.

The gifts of the Holy Spirit are given instantaneously and freely without merit. The growth of the human spirit takes intentional time and cultivation.

Any new believer can function in the manifestations of the Spirit because they are given freely. Yet, a mature believer functioning in the same gift will have a depth in execution and delivery that only comes from experience and familiarity with the flow of the Spirit.

For example, the manifestation of words of wisdom should not be confused with the wisdom that all believers have access to by asking the Father (James 1:5)—or even the spiritual wisdom that Paul prayed would come on the Ephesian believers (Eph. 1:17). Similarly, the manifestation of words of knowledge should not be confused with the knowledge of God that can be multiplied (2 Pet. 1:2-3).

The discerning of spirits is a spiritual manifestation that sees into the spiritual realm, but discernment is a result of us "abounding more and more" (Phil. 1:9).

The gifts of healings in First Corinthians 12 were not the command to lay hands on the sick that was given to all believers in Mark 16:18. One is an explosion of healing power by the move of the Spirit, while the other is a step of faith offered to all believers. Clearly not all elders in the Church had to have gifts of healings to qualify to serve as an elder, but all elders were expected to pray for the sick as called upon (James 5:14).

The gift of faith is an instantaneous infusion of supernatural faith. This is clearly different from the faith that comes by hearing (Rom. 10:17).

The spiritual manifestations spoken of in First Corinthians 12 flow from the Holy Spirit through our human spirits. But as our born-again human spirit grows in our walk with God, our spiritual senses are sharpened (Heb. 5:12-14).

We need both levels of operation and manifestation. We need the grace gifts of the Spirit because we can never earn those, but we also need to grow in our understanding of the Spirit because that is how we become skilled in our use of those gifts. We need to know how to operate from our spirit man, but we also need to know how to yield our spirit man to the higher leadings of the Holy Spirit. One leads to another.

The foundation of moving in any of the manifestations of the Holy Spirit is the human spirit. The more our spirit man is trained and tuned to the spiritual realm, the easier it will be to yield to the Holy Spirit's prompting.

> *"For God is my witness, whom I serve with my spirit in the gospel of His Son, that without ceasing I make mention of you always in my prayers."*
>
> ROMANS 1:9

> *"For I long to see you, that I may impart to you some spiritual gift, so that you may be established."*
>
> ROMANS 1:11

Paul understood that the yielding of his human spirit by serving God would lead to his desire and ability to impart spiritual gifts to the Roman believers.

A SPIRIT-INSPIRED CLASSIFICATION

"For to one is given the word of wisdom through the Spirit, to another the word of knowledge through the same Spirit, to another faith by the same Spirit, to another gifts of healings by the same Spirit, to another the working of miracles, to another prophecy, to another discerning of spirits, to another different kinds of tongues, to another the interpretation of tongues."

1 CORINTHIANS 12: 8-10

Rev. Howard Carter was a British Pentecostal pioneer who was active in ministry until he went to his heavenly reward in the mid-twentieth century. He was a conscientious objector in World War 1, and as result, was confined to prison for the term of the war. It was while he was in prison that the Lord revealed to him the division and classification of the nine gifts. The revelation was so profound that to this day, it is maintained as the standard that most ministers use to teach on the gifts. The Lord showed him these three key principles:

- There are three gifts of revelation: The word of wisdom, the word of knowledge, and the discerning of spirits.
- There are three gifts of power: The gift of faith, the gifts of healings, and the working of miracles.

- There are three gifts of inspiration: The gift of prophecy, the gift of tongues, and the interpretation of tongues.

The number three is God's number of divine perfection. God is Father, Son, and Holy Spirit. Man is spirit, soul, and body (1 Thess. 5:23). It would make sense, then, that the gifts of the Spirit also fall nicely into three categories of three.

- The three gifts of revelation reveal to man an element from the mind of God.
- The three gifts of power demonstrate to man an element of the strength and might of God.
- The three gifts of inspiration reveal to man God's edification, exhortation, and comfort.

Often these gifts work in unison with each other—sometimes so closely it becomes difficult to tell where one starts and the other ends.

Often these gifts work in unison with each other—sometimes so closely it becomes difficult to tell where one starts and the other ends.

These studies have helped me scripturally become quick to recognize the flow of the Spirit. It gave me a confidence to step out and yield to these anointings whenever they presented themselves. Studying along these lines has increased my faith for manifestations. And faith—for anything—comes by hearing what the Word of God has to say (Rom. 10:17).

Chapter One

THE WORD OF WISDOM

"…For to one is given the word of wisdom through the Spirit.…"

1 CORINTHIANS 12:8

The first of the gifts we'll look at is the gift of the word of wisdom.

Sophia (Strong's 4678), the Greek word translated as *wisdom* here, literally means *broad and full of intelligence, the knowledge of diverse matters, the act of interpreting dreams and giving the sagest advice, discovering the meaning of the mysterious, skill in the management of affairs, the wisdom of God in forming and executing the counsels in the formation and government of the world.*

Vine's expository dictionary says that *sophia* is the insight into *the true nature of things.*

So, you could say that the word *sophia* means "intelligent and full of insight into the true nature of things." While man sees the present and is fearful or unsure of the future, this manifestation unveils what the true nature and outcome of a circumstance is or will be.

The word of wisdom is a supernatural portion of the fore-knowledge of God into future events. It is a divine unveiling of divine purposes to come. It is a heavenly communication to the Church or to individuals. Through this gift, we receive a segment from the immense library of God's wisdom.

Wisdom has to do with the unknown, the future. Through this gift, God maps out His future plans for us. God's mind is revealed.

As with all the gifts, the word of wisdom has nothing to do with man's wisdom, which can be acquired through a variety of means including education, observation, and coaching. Also, man *does* have natural talents and gifts, but that is not what we are considering in this study.

As with all the gifts, the word of wisdom has nothing to do with man's wisdom.

This is also not the wisdom you get from God by asking Him as instructed in James 3:15. That is wisdom that God grants you for the affairs of life as you ask Him.

I have had people say to me, "Pastor, please pray for me. I need the wisdom of God." What they mean is that they need more insight and understanding into life. James 3:15 would be a perfect base for your prayer for this type of wisdom. As I have said, this manifestation, like all others in this category, is not the type of wisdom, either of spiritual or natural things, that you must grow into.

The word of wisdom goes beyond all generalities because it is a specific *word* from the vastness of God's wisdom. No one man could contain all of God's wisdom. Actually, no one man could contain all of *any* part of God.

Finite man cannot encompass all of infinite God. We can have all of Him that we want, but we must know that all we want is not all He has to give. We can have a portion of Him but not all of Him. So it is with these gifts; we only receive a *word* or a portion of what He actually is.

The word of wisdom is having the true nature of things revealed to you. Not just things as they appear, but as they will be in the future.

> *"Therefore the wisdom of God also said, 'I will send them prophets and apostles, and some of them they will kill and persecute,'"*
> LUKE 11:49

The wisdom of God speaks into the future. As we see here, it was the wisdom of God that spoke of sending prophets and apostles knowing that some would be martyred. This is important to know about the word of wisdom: it only deals with the future.

This was the gift in operation through which every Old Testament prophet spoke of the coming purposes of God in the earth. True prophetic utterance is a portion of the mind of

God concerning things to come. For that reason, it has been said accurately that the word of wisdom should be the most coveted of the gifts. It is certainly the best of the gifts to operate in.

THE WORD OF WISDOM OR THE WORD OF KNOWLEDGE

We will look at the word of knowledge in our next chapter, but it would help us to note the similarities and differences here because many times these gifts will operate concurrently. It is almost impossible to completely separate words of wisdom and knowledge since they are operations, which is actually true for all nine gifts. As we study the gifts, we will see that to isolate them independently would be almost impossible— not to mention unnecessary. The lines of delineation between the nine operations cannot be clearly drawn. They flow seamlessly between and into one another.

This is not unusual with the things of God; this is actually the case with most branches of scriptural study. One of the basic rules of studying systematic theology or Bible doctrines is to understand that no single doctrine can stand alone. So, if you were studying soteriology (the doctrine of salvation) you would invariably also have to have an understanding of Christology (the doctrine of Christ) because how could you understand salvation if you did not know who Jesus is? There is an intermingling of all things God. He designed it that way.

The main difference between the word of knowledge and the word of wisdom is that the word of knowledge always deals with current or past information, whereas the word of wisdom is always looking into the future, revealing what we need to do with that information and what the outcomes will be. Proverbs 15:2 sums it up nicely:

"The tongue of the wise uses knowledge rightly."

Many people have knowledge, but it doesn't do anything to add to their lives. For many years, I would head up medical outreaches to third-world countries. I would gather an international team of medically trained personnel and fly into many places where there was not running water or electricity. Many times in those places, we would purchase our supplies locally at pharmacies or hospitals. One time, as we drove to the hospital to get more supplies, I chanced upon a group of doctors and nurses standing outside the hospital, taking a smoke break. The funny thing was that they were standing under a sign that clearly said, "Smoking Kills."

I am sure that as medically trained personals, they knew the health risks involved in smoking. But they were standing under a sign that proclaimed that none of their knowledge did anything for them.

THE GIFT OF THE WORD OF WISDOM

Every prophetic utterance by Old Testament prophets was a result of the word of wisdom in operation. The word of wisdom deals in the hidden things, and this is true for any prophecy that is uttered today.

> Every prophetic utterance by Old Testament prophets was a result of the word of wisdom in operation.

This is the gift that anyone seeking out psychics, clairvoyants, or horoscopes is actually looking for. Like all the other gifts, this can change the world.

Since prophecy plays such a major role in the Bible, the word of wisdom is in operation all through the Word. Here are a few examples of this gift in the Old Testament.

NOAH SURVIVES THE FLOOD THROUGH THE WORD OF WISDOM

"And God said to Noah, 'The end of all flesh has come before Me, for the earth is filled with violence through them; and behold, I will destroy them with the earth. And behold, I Myself am bringing floodwaters on the earth, to destroy from under heaven all flesh in which is the breath of life; everything that is on the earth shall die.'"

GENESIS 6:13,17

"For after seven more days I will cause it to rain on the earth forty days and forty nights, and I will destroy from the face of the earth all living things that I have made."

GENESIS 7:4

Noah knew a flood was coming way before it actually occurred, and he knew what the results would be. Noah did not have any human way to guess that God would flood the earth. The word of wisdom warned him of impending danger, and it also provided a way of escape.

Many years back, an area in Asia where I had ministered for many years experienced severe flooding. Lives were lost and churches destroyed. Shortly after the damage, I was contacted by some of the pastors that I work with in that region. They called because two women had started telling people that as they were praying, they had a vision of Jesus. He was crying over the lives lost in the flood. The pastors wanted to know what I thought about this vision.

"That vision was not God," I told them. "God never warns us *after* a tragedy. His mercy dictates that He warn us before. What does such a vision do for anyone now?"

I've also had people tell me about a dream or premonition they had that told them something bad was about to occur. One such couple told me that for six months the wife would have a recurring dream of them in a car wreck. And, sure enough, one day they were in a wreck just like she had been dreaming about for six months.

After the accident, they said to me, "God told us that this would happen, so it must be His will."

I answered, "You are right that God told you, but the reason He told you was so that you could pray and take authority over it. Why would He tell you that you were about to have a car wreck and leave you to stew in fear for six months? No! He told you so that you could have a way out, but you took it as a prediction instead of a warning and became fearful instead of believing for deliverance."

The word of wisdom is not meant to spread dread and fear of the future. It might tell us of destruction to come, but if it does, it will always include a way of escape

MOSES ANSWERS THE PEOPLE'S COMPLAINTS THROUGH THE WORD OF WISDOM

"I have heard the complaints of the children of Israel. Speak to them, saying, 'At twilight you shall eat meat, and in the morning you shall be filled with bread. And you shall know that I am the Lord your God.'"

EXODUS 16:12

Since Moses was such a major figure in the Old Testament, there were many other occurrences where he had this gift manifest through him. But I wanted you to see that not only can this gift operate on a national scale like with Noah, but it can also operate on a smaller scale like with the next meal the children of Israel were going to have.

The word of wisdom brings hope that the next morning can be vastly different from the previous night. Like everything else that God does, there is always an underlying theme of fear not. Beware of prophetic words that breed fear or doom. All prophetic utterances that come from God will carry the heart of God.

ELIJAH DECLARES AN END TO A DROUGHT THROUGH THE WORD OF WISDOM

"Then Elijah said to Ahab, 'Go up, eat and drink; for there is the sound of abundance of rain.'"

1 KINGS 18:41

After a spectacular victory over the prophets of Baal, Elijah prophesied an end to the drought that God had prophesied *through* Elijah in First Kings 17. Elijah had said that the rain would only return at his command. This was a prophecy coming full circle. As with all true spiritual gifts in operation, there was nothing in the natural to suggest this would happen anytime soon. But the word of wisdom speaks into the future.

Not only was there not a physical sign of a cloud for Elijah to see, the word he had received also came without physical sound. It was an internal sound audible only to his spirit man. He was hearing in the spirit and speaking by faith. If you do not see and hear on the inside, you will never dare speak and possess on the outside.

Elijah *heard* rain. Elijah *heard* this word of wisdom. Any of the gifts can operate in more than one way. We must always expect a diversity in how the gifts manifest. Even within the manifestation of the same gift, there are a multiplicity of ways that it can operate.

ELISHA PROPHESIED ECONOMIC MARKETS THROUGH THE WORD OF WISDOM

"Then Elisha said, 'Hear the word of the Lord. Thus says the Lord: Tomorrow about this time a seah of fine

flour shall be sold for a shekel, and two seahs of barley for a shekel, at the gate of Samaria.'"

2 KINGS 7:1

Since Elisha received a double portion of Elijah's anointing, it would be no surprise to us that he also operated in the word of wisdom like Elijah. Relationships play a major role in impartations and anointings. There is a principle of deep calling unto deep that is involved in stirring the gifts on the inside of us.

In the previous chapter in 2 Kings, dung had been sold for much more than a single shekel, so to declare that flour and barley would once again be available to the common person was indeed a bold statement.

God wasn't just speaking about the price of groceries at the local supermarket; He was demonstrating that He can inform us of how the economic markets of the world will turn. Imagine what this would do for business people.

All the gifts mentioned in First Corinthians 12 are meant to profit us (1 Cor. 12:7). Obviously, profit isn't limited to finances but surely to profit us must include finances.

DAVID DESCRIBED THE CRUCIFIXION THROUGH THE WORD OF WISDOM

David was a king, warrior, and psalmist. Many of his psalms took a prophetic turn as he started prophesying about the coming Messiah.

Psalm 22 is a good example of this.

"My God, My God, why have You forsaken Me? Why are You so far from helping Me and from the words of My groaning?"

PSALM 22:1

David not only described the intense feelings of Jesus on the cross, he described it so vividly that Jesus actually repeated those same words while He was on the cross.

David likely did not know that he was prophesying about what Jesus would experience, but since it is only a word of wisdom, David was just receiving a word about the ministry of Jesus!

Later on, in the same psalm, David caught a glimpse of the Roman soldiers' treatment of Jesus before the crucifixion (John 19:24; Matthew 27:35). This exact scenario was acted out by the gentile soldiers who could in no way know they were fulfilling prophecy.

"They divide My garments among them, and for My clothing they cast lots."

PSALM 22:18

So we can see from this that like David with Jesus, not only can the word of wisdom put you in someone else's frame of mind—like with the Roman soldiers—it can also describe what people are going to do in detail.

"He will glorify Me, for He will take of what is Mine and declare it to you."

JOHN 16:14

The word of wisdom, like all the other gifts, is a vehicle through which an aspect of Jesus is revealed.

The word of wisdom, like all the other gifts, is a vehicle through which an aspect of Jesus is revealed. The Holy Spirit's main mission is to reveal Jesus to us. Since the gifts are expressions of the Holy Spirit, and since the Holy Spirit's mandate is to reveal Jesus, it would make sense that the gifts of the Spirit reveal Jesus to us.

> "...No one can say that Jesus is Lord except by the Holy Spirit."
>
> 1 CORINTHIANS 12:3

Again, any spiritual gift in demonstration that does not point us to Jesus as Lord over our circumstances is not from the Holy Spirit.

I remember once being told of a minster who held crusades internationally. He would call people out and claim that by the Spirit he could tell them their sins and wrongs. That's against spiritual protocol. The gifts are never meant to embarrass or expose people. They are meant to uplift people by showing them Jesus. There are situations where error and sin are exposed by the Spirit, but it is always to protect believers and the Church, never to humiliate. Such prophecies, if to bring correction and call for personal repentance, should always be done in private with mature witnesses to judge the utterance.

Jesus is always elevated when the gifts are in proper operation.

DANIEL SAW KINGDOMS TO COME THROUGH THE WORD OF WISDOM

"But after you shall arise another kingdom inferior to yours; then another, a third kingdom of bronze, which shall rule over all the earth."

DANIEL 2:39

Daniel had a far-reaching prophetic ministry. He did not just have insight into the current affairs of his day, but he also had revelation about kingdoms to come and end-time events. For example, King Nebuchadnezzar had a dream that he couldn't remember, but he still demanded an interpretation. Daniel not only told him the details of the dream, but he also had the prophetic interpretation. The interpretation spoke of kingdoms to come after King Nebuchadnezzar's reign. Through the gift of the word of wisdom, Daniel later saw the end times.

The truth is that besides everything that we know the Bible is, it is primarily a book of fulfilled, and yet to be fulfilled, prophecies. There are an estimated 8,362 predictive verses and 1,817 predictions on 737 separate matters[1].

The Old Testament contains over 300 prophecies about the coming Messiah. Jesus fulfilled every one of those prophecies in His first coming. No other religious text from any "ism" even comes close to the Bible's track record of prophetic

---

1   J. Barton Payne, Encyclopedia of Biblical Prophecy

accuracy. The Bible stands alone in this regard. The gift of the word wisdom is the reason.

We've seen how the word of wisdom ministers both to individuals and corporately to the Church at large, But there is also an aspect of the word of wisdom that speaks not just to nations and kingdoms but also to the end of time itself. The word of wisdom reaches into eternity.

JOEL SAW THE OUTPOURING OF THE SPIRIT THROUGH THE WORD OF WISDOM

Outside of the crucifixion, perhaps the most important event in the New Testament is the outpouring of the Holy Spirit on the day of Pentecost.

The crucifixion got us into the Body of Christ, but the outpouring of the Spirit put the fullness of the Spirit into us!

What happened in the upper room to the 120 disciples was vividly described through the word of wisdom delivered by the prophet Joel:

> *"And it shall come to pass afterward that I will pour out My Spirit on all flesh; your sons and your daughters shall prophesy, your old men shall dream dreams, your young men shall see visions. And also on My menservants and on My maidservants I will pour out My Spirit in those days."*
>
> JOEL 2:28-29

Consider that in the time of Joel, the idea of the Holy Spirit being poured out on all flesh was an outlandish concept. It would have been plausible if the prophecy said the Spirit would be poured out on kings and priests, maybe even on some of the Hebrew leaders, but *all* flesh? This was foreign in the Jewish ideology of the day. Yet that was what was spoken through the word of wisdom, and it was exactly what happened in Acts 2.

ISAIAH SAW THE MESSIAH'S SUFFERING THROUGH THE WORD OF WISDOM

Perhaps the most vivid Old Testament description of Jesus as the suffering servant comes from Isaiah. Through the entirety of chapter 53, it sounds as if Isaiah steps into the footprints of Jesus through His trial and crucifixion. The description is so graphic that it reads like a running commentary of the actual events.

Obviously, Isaiah neither knew the full weight of what he was seeing into, nor did he live to see the fulfilment of his prophetic utterance. Yet, centuries later, we can all read in awe of the accurate detail in his word of wisdom.

THE WORD OF WISDOM COMES THROUGH DREAMS

Since part of *sophia* is the interpreting of dreams, it should come as no surprise that prophetic foretelling through dreams is a common occurrence in the Bible.

A seventeen-year-old Joseph saw the unfolding of his remarkable life through a dream (Gen. 37). None of his family members believed in his dreams, but that did not stop what God showed him from coming to pass. It would stand to reason that Joseph himself had many occasions to forget what he saw in his dreams. Having his brothers bow before him and being a leader was surely an image that Joseph had to intentionally hold onto when he was sold into slavery and then made a servant. That was surely one of the reasons God revealed the future to Joseph—not just for predictive purposes but to keep the vision in the front of his mind during dark times. The word of wisdom keeps the lamp of hope alive.

There are many people who have had a glimpse of God's plan and purpose for their futures, but their current situations do not resemble that hope in any way. We must hold on to what God has shown us. Life was not all perfect for Joseph just because he received a dream from God. If anything, it all went downhill from there. But the dream left Joseph with a spark of hope that he could attach his faith to. If what you are currently experiencing does not match what you have been shown by God, know that what and where God intends you to be is still ahead of you.

What God showed you through the word of wisdom is just part of the journey. Do not park there. Keep moving!

What God showed you through the word of wisdom by prophecy, dreams, or visons is always in the future tense. You are heading toward it, and any contrary landscape you are traveling over is just part of the journey. Do not park there. Keep moving!

THE WORD OF WISDOM CAN ALSO COME BY AN AUDIBLE VOICE

"Now Samuel did not yet know the Lord, nor was the word of the Lord yet revealed to him."

1 SAMUEL 3:7

One remarkable account of the word of wisdom in operation was through an audible voice heard by a young Samuel. Since we are explicitly told that Samuel had no relationship with God at this point, we can conclude that this was an audible voice—at least to Samuel—since he repeatedly thought it was his master, Eli, calling him. Interestingly, not only did the voice call out to Samuel by name, but when he followed the advice of Eli and allowed the voice to speak to him, it told him of the impending judgment to befall Eli and his household (1 Sam. 3 :11-14).

We can all rejoice here to see that not only does God know those who do not yet know Him by name, but that the operations of the Spirit can take place through anyone. This undergirds that "...the gifts and calling of God are irrevocable" (Rom. 11:29). The manifestations of the Spirit are freely given.

JESUS AND THE WORD OF WISDOM

"And so also were James and John, the sons of Zebedee, who were partners with Simon. And Jesus said to

Simon, 'Do not be afraid. From now on you will catch
men.'"

LUKE 5:10

The simple phrase, "From now on you will catch men" was a word of wisdom that not only changed the lives of Peter, James, and John but countless others.

The disciples called to ministry, and ultimately apostleship, started with a prophetic pronouncement. Certainly, all twelve of the disciples were similarly called, but these three were a most unlikely group.

In a sense, any call to ministry has an element of the word of wisdom to it; most calls to ministry have an element of entering something that is in the future. So, you could say that the word of wisdom calls a person to ministry. Even if they are not called to a pulpit-type, public speaking ministry, the truth is that all believers have a call to the plan of God. This call can be demonstrated in many ways—from the type of career a youth aspires to where someone may feel called to move. These are elements of the leading of the Spirit, but they usually have an aspect of the word of wisdom in them.

JESUS' WORD OF WISDOM ABOUT TROUBLES TO COME

The word of wisdom through Jesus did not just call individuals; in some cases, it brought warnings as well. This is a powerful aspect of the gift: to warn us of the enemy's plans.

And Jesus answered and said to them: "Take heed that
no one deceives you. For many will come in My name,

saying, "I am the Christ," and will deceive many. And you will hear of wars and rumors of wars. See that you are not troubled; for all these things must come to pass, but the end is not yet. For nation will rise against nation, and kingdom against kingdom. And there will be famines, pestilences, and earthquakes in various places."

MATTHEW 24:4-7

These particular predictions by Jesus (all through the rest of Matthew 24) went beyond the personal foretelling aspects of the word of wisdom and brought us all into what will ultimately be the signs of the end of the age. We see that not only was personal instruction given, but the entire age was summed up. "He who endures to the end..." (Matt. 24:13).

THE WORD OF WISDOM THROUGH ANANIAS, AN EVERYDAY DISCIPLE

"Now there was a certain disciple at Damascus named Ananias; and to him the Lord said in a vision, 'Ananias.' And he said, 'Here I am, Lord.'"

ACTS 9:10

"But the Lord said to him, 'Go, for he is a chosen vessel of Mine to bear My name before Gentiles, kings, and the children of Israel.'"

ACTS 9:15

I love that this passage shows us that an everyday disciple, not in the top tier of Church leadership, yielded to the Spirit and was used by God to assist and activate Saul into what we would ultimately become the farthest reaching ministry from the early Church. I love that by the ministry of the Holy Spirit through us, we have potential to touch individuals from all spheres of life.

Years ago, I was invited to take a tour of the administrative headquarters of a very old and established denomination. They preached a solid salvation message and had planted many churches because of it.

Over time, though, things had become stale, and many of the leaders and churches had gotten away from the fire that the movement had started with. I've discovered that revelation is never secondhand; it must be fresh to every generation. These particular brethren, who had once blazed with evangelistic zeal, had never fully embraced the outpouring of the Spirit that had come to that region through the charismatic movement in the 1960s. The effect of missing out on all that the Spirit offered was being slowly, but surely, seen throughout the organization.

As I walked around the huge campus, someone recognized me and offered me the chance to meet the president and vice president of the denomination, both of whom happened to be present that day. I readily agreed, and within a short time, was ushered into a massive meeting room with an equally large boardroom table in the middle of it.

In a short time, the president, vice president, and an administrator of their theological seminary came walking in. They were polite and cordial, showing a genuine interest in me. They knew I was a Spirit-filled minister and soon the conversation turned to the present-day ministry of the Holy

Spirit. They asked sincere questions, but it was obvious that it was really the administrator of the seminary who was truly hungry for the move of the Spirit.

We conversed for about forty-five minutes, and as we were getting ready to leave, they asked if I would pray to close the meeting. We all bowed our heads as I led in prayer. I was planning to keep to protocol and pray a heartfelt but "denominational" prayer, but halfway through, I sensed the anointing come into the room. I specifically felt that there was a word that needed to be released over the administrator.

They were all seated on the opposite end of the large boardroom table and were nowhere near me. I did not want to draw attention to myself by getting up halfway through the prayer and walking over to him, so I just moved the flow of prayer toward him by asking God to bless him and increase in him. As I was praying, I peeked open one eye and saw that he was quietly crying under the anointing. Just when I thought I was finished praying for him, an utterance suddenly came forth that included the phrase, "You will be promoted and positioned to open doors for the flow of the Spirit."

As I finished praying, everyone else stood to leave, but the administrator remained seated for a while longer. I sensed the anointing was still on him strongly. About eighteen months later, I heard that through a series of unusual events, this administrator had received an unexpected number of votes at a denominational election and was installed as the vice president of the denomination. True to the desires of his heart and the word of wisdom released that day, he opened the doors for a more Spirit-friendly curriculum in the denomination's seminaries. I've heard that many have received the baptism of the Spirit's fullness since he was placed in office. The word of wisdom pointed him out and foretold what he would do with and for the Spirit of God.

Chapter Two

THE WORD OF KNOWLEDGE

"…To another the word of knowledge through the same Spirit."

1 Corinthians 12:8

This is one of my favorite manifestations because I have seen how it opens the door to so many of the other operations in my own life. But it should be recognized that of all the nine manifestations listed in First Corinthians 12, the word of knowledge requires the most scriptural mining to ponder its definition and scope. I think this is because it is a manifestation that covers such a vast mode of delivery. It truly is a manifestation that has a "diversity of operation" (1 Cor. 12:6 KJV).

Gnosis (Strong's 1108), the Greek word used here, signifies *knowledge* in intelligence and understanding. Vine's Expository Dictionary defines *gnosis* as *seeking to know, especially of spiritual truth*.

Gnosis comes from *ghinoceko* (Strong's 1097), which means *to know, allow, be aware of, feel, perceived, understand, to be acquainted with.* Of this word, Vine's Expository Dictionary says, *"to be taking in knowledge, to come to know, recognize, to understand completely."*

The word of knowledge and the previously discussed word of wisdom are almost twin operations—they will often function together. But then, all the manifestations have a way of intermingling so that sometimes it is nearly impossible to see where one ends and the other begins. There is a seamless, divine unity among all nine manifestations. Our purpose in looking at them individually is simply for the ease of studying, clarity, and definitions, but they seldom function independently. I guess you could say the same about the Trinity as well. The Father, Son, and Holy Spirit all work in unison.

The word of knowledge is the supernatural unveiling from the vast storehouse of the mind of God concerning facts in heaven and earth.

The word of knowledge is the supernatural unveiling from the vast storehouse of the mind of God concerning facts in heaven and earth. Since God knows every person, place, and situation, the word of knowledge deals with events that are or have happened.

Since God dwells in an eternal, ongoing "now," this is not a divine recall of memory; all time—past, present, and future—is ever before Him. Since all events in time are before God, all events are knowledge to Him. The word of knowledge is a revelation to man, by the Spirit regarding specific details from that "all-knowledge."

Simply put, the word of knowledge is a revelation of facts. It deals with what exists—present or past. This would include conversations, historical events, thoughts, and emotions.

The word of knowledge is a delight to see in operation. It never fails to get the attention of the person receiving the word because it reveals things about him or her that the believer delivering the word couldn't have known. And if delivered publicly, the word will always bring an awe to those witnessing its operation.

One of my favorite memories of this manifestation in operation was when I was new to these gifts and was actively pursuing them (though I still do). A lady who was new to my ministry asked to see me after a service one day. She was an older woman and was wanting to invest her retirement money. There were three possible offers in front of her, and she was seeking the will of God concerning which to take.

Now, let me say that as New Testament believers, we do not need to seek out prophets or prophecy for direction because we have access to God's Word and the Holy Spirit 24/7. But we can certainly solicit prayer and counsel for decisions we need to make. It was in this manner that she sought me out.

As we were talking, she reached into her purse and pulled out a calling card of one of the men who had approached her with the business. What happened next surprised me.

As I reached out to take the card from her, I suddenly saw the man who gave the card. I saw his facial features. As I described them to the woman, she excitedly confirmed that that was exactly how he looked. Then I "heard" and "sensed" his business acumen and temperaments. As I have said, there is a diversity in the ways that the gifts can manifest and none more so than the word of knowledge.

The word of knowledge brings out a tiny slice of the omniscience of God.

Among many other things, I told her that he was quick to make decisions and recklessly impetuous. She agreed that she had sensed that about him as well. She quickly took out the second and third calling cards from the other business opportunities and handed them to me. As I reached out to take each card, I saw, heard, and sensed each of the men involved. Obviously, I had never met any of them, and until meeting the lady, I had never even heard of their business ventures. I did not make any business decisions for the woman, I simply told her what I sensed from each opportunity. She confirmed each time that she had felt the same about them. Having the Lord so beautifully confirm what she sensed freed her to make the decision she needed.

The word of knowledge brings out a tiny slice of the omniscience of God. It never reveals everything, but usually it reveals just enough to get our attention and lift us so we can make a choice.

While all believers have access to these manifestations, both the word of wisdom and the word of knowledge will manifest with more regularity and intensity for those called to the office of the prophet (Eph. 4:11). Both of these manifestations make up the revealing, predictive, foretelling elements of the supernatural ministries you see anywhere in scripture— Old Testament prophetic occurrences to the ministries of Jesus and the early Church.

THE WORD OF KNOWLEDGE ENCOURAGED ELIJAH

We see in First Kings 19 that having just defeated 450 prophets of Baal at Mount Carmel, Elijah immediately folded before facing the wrath of the evil queen Jezebel—a woman who basically ordered hitmen to have Elijah assassinated.

Having just come from the miraculous victory on Mount Carmel, Elijah, was physically tired and fell into depression. It is important for us to know that because we are a spirit, soul, and body, what affects us in one area has the potential of affecting our other parts. Balance is key to maintain any victory. Elijah was physically tired and that led to him falling into despair. He conquered 450 prophets of Baal singlehandedly but then cowered before one women.

> *And he said, 'I have been very zealous for the Lord God of hosts; because the children of Israel have forsaken Your covenant, torn down Your altars, and*

killed Your prophets with the sword. I alone am left;
and they seek to take my life.'

1 KINGS 19:14

In his depression, Elijah concluded that he was the only person true to God and that he would soon lose his life. Clearly, this was a victim mentality speaking; he had been the sole opposer of the 450 prophets of Baal and had come out victorious. It is feasible to conclude that in this state of depression, he would not have even bothered trying to oppose or escape any of Jezebel's men if they found him. Yet even in this depleted state, God spoke to him: "...Yet I have reserved *seven thousand* in Israel, all whose knees have not bowed to Baal, and every mouth that has not kissed him" (1 Kings 19:18).

Seven thousand Israelites had not pledged allegiance to Baal, but in the natural, Elijah could not, and did not, know that.

The word of knowledge can reveal facts unknown to you. The word of knowledge gave Elijah *an accurate picture of current circumstances* so that he no longer had to operate under his own depressing assumptions. When faced with challenges, the word of knowledge can cut through the clutter and shine light on what is true.

THE WORD OF KNOWLEDGE IN THE MINISTRY OF ELISHA

Elisha, Elijah's successor, had many remarkable manifestations of the word of knowledge in his lifetime. In fact, he had more occurrences of the word of knowledge functioning through him than any other person in the Old Testament.

"But Gehazi, the servant of Elisha the man of God, said, 'Look, my master has spared Naaman this Syrian, while not receiving from his hands what he brought; but as the Lord lives, I will run after him and take something from him.'"

2 KINGS 5:20

Naaman was a Syrian general that had received a healing miracle through the ministry of Elisha. Out of gratitude, he had offered Elisha monetary gifts. Elisha declined the gifts, but his servant, Gehazi, evidently heard of this offer and decided to go behind his master's back to Naaman.

"And he said, 'All is well. My master has sent me, saying, 'Indeed, just now two young men of the sons of the prophets have come to me from the mountains of Ephraim. Please give them a talent of silver and two changes of garments.'"

2 KINGS 5:22

Catching up to Naaman, Gehazi made up a noble lie. He said money was needed for others in need and that he was collecting for them. It is ironic that even though he was around the miraculous ministry of Elisha, he did not have enough of the fear of God to think anything of this outright lie. Being around the supernatural doesn't allow the supernatural in and through you unless you intentionally allow it. Impartations only come when you are purposefully cooperating with the anointing. Naaman innocently gave, and Gehazi happily received more than was requested.

"Now he went in and stood before his master. Elisha said to him, 'Where did you go, Gehazi?' And he said, 'Your servant did not go anywhere.'"

2 KINGS 5:25

Returning, Gehazi was gently confronted by Elisha. I suspect that by that point the word of knowledge had already been given to Elisha about Gehazi. The manifestations of the Spirit are never meant to function outside of the heart of the Father, which is love and mercy. I am convinced that no further verses would have been recorded had Gehazi simply confessed to Elisha. But sadly, as it is with many who have given themselves over to a lifestyle of falsehoods, Gehazi could not stop himself so that he could see the mercy of God being offered to him.

"Then he said to him, 'Did not my heart go with you when the man turned back from his chariot to meet you? Is it time to receive money and to receive clothing, olive groves and vineyards, sheep and oxen, male and female servants?'"

2 KINGS 5:26

Elisha's description of how he knew where Gehazi was is priceless for our study. Notice how Elisha said that "his heart went with him." This was symbolically saying that it was as if Elisha himself had been present at the exchange. We've already noted that the word of knowledge can manifest as something you see, hear, or even feel, but it can also manifest as if a person is transported to a certain location or event.

Gehazi had only received silver from Naaman, but I believe Elisha had a further word of knowledge of what Gehazi had intended to do with the silver. He intended to buy "...clothing, olive groves and vineyards, sheep and oxen, male and female servants."

Obviously, with such power on display and with such a lack of reverence on Gehazi's part, this account did not end well. Elisha allowed him to keep the silver but pronounced that the leprosy previously on Naaman would now plague Gehazi.

SAME MANIFESTATION, DIFFERENT TIME

There is a similar account of how the word of knowledge functioned to maintain the integrity of the ministry in Acts 5.

Ananias and Sapphira, a couple in the early Church, decided to sell some real estate and give a portion of the proceeds to the apostles. This was their right to do since it was never commanded that disciples give all their belongings to the Church. However, what they decided to do was to report that they brought *all* the proceeds to the Church. Clearly, their goal was to achieve status within the Church with this show of generosity.

On the cross, we see the mercy and the judgment of God in simultaneous fullness.

Sadly, like Gehazi, Ananias and Sapphire were so caught up in their lies that they blindly failed to see that God is always merciful and just. There is no clearer picture of this than the crucifixion of Jesus. On the cross, we see the mercy and the judgment of God in simultaneous fullness. You can easily conclude that Ananias and Sapphira had developed an ongoing lifestyle of dishonesty because no one would start out lying on such a grand scale. It's the small foxes that ruin the vine (Song of Sol. 2:15).

Obviously, there have been many who have lied in the Church since Ananias and Sapphira and not died immediately. There were clearly unique circumstances that resulted in their immediate deaths. As such, this passage of scripture can not be used as a standard for all people who lie in church. Church doctrine or standards can only be established when there is more than one supporting scripture in the New Testament, but it obviously was recorded for our benefit like all biblical accounts.

We see throughout Scripture that God's chastisement of His children is never punitive, but always corrective. This fits into the picture of the Father's heart toward us.

Thus, we are left with the possibility that Ananias and Sapphira were either not believers to begin with or had chosen to become reprobate believers in spite of the light available to them. Regardless, at this infant stage of the Church, there was such flow of purity and power among the believers that this infraction could not go unpunished.

The word of knowledge could have corrected and saved Ananias and Sapphira. Their deaths were mercy-oriented—both toward them as well as the Church—to maintain a standard of purity. It was not the word of knowledge that caused their deaths, just like it was not the word of knowledge that caused Gehazi's leprosy. It was the refusal to accept God's offer of mercy that led to their collective demise.

THE WORD OF KNOWLEDGE EXPOSES A KING'S PLANS

"And one of his servants said, 'None, my lord, O king; but Elisha, the prophet who is in Israel, tells the king of Israel the words that you speak in your bedroom.'"

2 KINGS 6:12

The Syrian king (Ben Hadad II) was plotting an ambush against the people of God, but each time he tried, the prophet of God revealed his secret plans to King Jehoram. This happened numerous times. The word of knowledge through Elisha was sharp and clear. It was precise. The word of knowledge brings with it a clarity to what the enemy tries to hide.

Fear is always and only the result of uncertainty or an unmanifested expectation.

The works of the enemy can be exposed by the operations of the Spirit.

The word of knowledge can be the remedy to uncertainty. The works of the Enemy can be exposed by the operations of the Spirit. The manifestations of these gifts are weapons in our arsenal.

King Ben Hadad suspected a spy (possibly Naaman, one of his generals) but was informed that Jehoram had a better informant. He had access to "...Elisha, the prophet who is in Israel, tells the king of Israel the words that you speak in your bedroom" (2 Kings 6:12). The fame of Elisha, not only his healing ministry that drew Naaman but also his prophetic insights, had spread all the way to Syria.

The plans of the enemy against you in any area of life can be thwarted by the operation of the word of knowledge.

> *"However, when He, the Spirit of truth, has come, He will guide you into all truth; for He will not speak on His own authority, but whatever He hears He will speak; and He will tell you things to come."*
>
> JOHN 16:13

I believe that this prophetic word of wisdom from Jesus about the then, soon coming of the Holy Spirit, in part, foretold of the Holy Spirit's utilization of the word of knowledge in guiding us into all (current) truth, as well as the word of wisdom telling of "things to come."

This is part of the Holy Spirit's ministry to us. One of the ways the Holy Spirit tells us things is through the gifts of the Spirit. The coming and indwelling of the Holy Spirit is also one of the reasons why Jesus said that it would be better for the disciples if He went away—so the Holy Spirit could come.

Like Elisha, we should be known abroad because of the Spirit's manifestations in and through us. I believe that the

Church is progressing and maturing to the place where these manifestations will operate so accurately that national and political events can be influenced for the things of God by the Church.

THE WORD OF KNOWLEDGE REVEALS A SECRET DREAM TO DANIEL

In our modern-day setting, you would not consider Daniel a preacher or a prophet. He lived in a secular, political surrounding, serving various heathen kings in mostly administrative positions. Yet he stayed true to God and had such mighty manifestations of the Spirit flow through him that years later, Jesus Himself quoted and pronounced Daniel a prophet (Matt. 24:15).

One beautiful feature of the manifestations of the Spirit are that they are not confined to "church" as we know and define it. They can operate perfectly outside of the buildings we call our churches. The gifts are given to believers, not to brick and mortar structures; this is so that wherever believers go, the gifts go with them. This scriptural idea alone gives credence to what we would call marketplace ministry and ministers.

The gifts are given to believers, not to brick and mortar structures, So wherever believers go, the gifts go with them.

I have always observed that if a person's gift only works on a Sunday morning, then we have a right to be suspicious of it.

Such was the case with Daniel. He was not a priest or a king and was not officially recognized as a prophet, but he functioned in the office of one and had the accompanying gifts in abundance. As believers, we should fully expect for the manifestations of the Spirit to accompany us wherever we are. This would include at home, at work, and any other setting we find ourselves in. The Holy Spirit and His manifestations cannot be confined to a building.

> "If you do not make known the dream to me, there is only one decree for you! For you have agreed to speak lying and corrupt words before me till the time has changed. Therefore, tell me the dream, and I shall know that you can give me its interpretation."
>
> DANIEL 2:9

Nebuchadnezzar, one of the four kings Daniel served in his lifetime, had an unusual demand. He had a disturbing dream, but rather than have the usual court soothsayers interpret it for him, he knew enough about them to distrust them. So, he cooked up a humanly impossible scenario. He did not just want his dream interpreted, he wanted them to tell him the dream he had in the first place. It always struck me as odd that he had so little trust in his own court soothsayers, yet he kept them around.

> "The Chaldeans answered the king, and said, 'There is not a man on earth who can tell the king's matter;

*therefore no king, lord, or ruler has ever asked such
things of any magician, astrologer, or Chaldean.'"*

DANIEL 2:10

*"For this reason the king was angry and very furious,
and gave the command to destroy all the wise men of
Babylon."*

DANIEL 2:12

Things reached a fever pitch as the Chaldean soothsayers declined the offer and enraged the king. Nebuchadnezzar
commanded what was common in those day when kings
did not get their way: he started having them executed. The
executions continued until they almost reached Daniel and
his companions.

*"Then with counsel and wisdom Daniel answered
Arioch, the captain of the king's guard, who had gone
out to kill the wise men of Babylon."*

DANIEL 2:14

Now, this is a point we have already looked at. Daniel
answered the captain of the king's guard with wisdom. It was
not the word of wisdom but just the wisdom that came from
Daniel's walk with God and his personal growth. There is a
clear demarcation as we have seen between the gifts given to
us and the growth that comes on us as we mature with God.
We need both gifts *and* growth.

From this position of wisdom needed to handle life, Daniel
asked the king for time to seek God and to have an answer
presented to him.

What a great picture of the natural leading to the supernatural! Daniel had "natural" wisdom that came from personal and spiritual maturity, and it led to the supernatural manifestation of the Spirit. We need both. Daniel would have missed out on the supernatural if he had not followed the flow of the natural.

You might say that it was just common sense that Daniel asked for more time to pray, but my years of ministry have taught me that the problem with commonsense is that it is not so common.

We can only use what we have in the natural with wisdom and then make room for the supernatural.

Since we are tripartite beings, there must come a harmony between the spirit, soul, and body. One leads to another. His wisdom in asking for the natural time led to the supernatural. We need not rush to the supernatural. Indeed, we cannot. We can only use what we have in the natural with wisdom and then make room for the supernatural.

> *"Then the secret was revealed to Daniel in a night vision. So Daniel blessed the God of heaven."*
> DANIEL 2:19

> *"I thank You and praise You, O God of my fathers; You have given me wisdom and might, and have now*

made known to me what we asked of You, for You have made known to us the king's demand."

DANIEL 2:23

Ironically, the secret of Nebuchadnezzar's dream was revealed to Daniel in a dream of his own. Many times the manifestations of the Spirit can come through the vehicle of dreams. Joseph, the earthly father of Jesus, experienced a word of knowledge through a dream where he was instructed to flee to Egypt (Matt. 2:13) with Mary and Jesus to escape Herod. The avenues that the gifts of the Spirit can flow through are endless.

Since the nine gifts all flow from the same Spirit, we can expect that the manifestation of one will often lead to the manifestation of another. The gifts don't just work in unity; they open up ways so that one leads to another.

God did not just give Daniel a word of knowledge of Nebuchadnezzar's dream. Through it, God also revealed a word of wisdom to interpret the future events from the dream. Daniel chapter 2 is a well-known biblical prophecy where Daniel goes on to declare the kingdoms to follow Nebuchadnezzar.

So, the word of knowledge revealing Nebuchadnezzar's dream led to the word of wisdom revealing the future.

There is divine synchronicity to the gifts in operation. God is always on the lookout for ways to give more to us. If we will allow one operation of the Spirit into our lives, it will quickly open the door for more to come in.

THE WORD OF KNOWLEDGE CAN COME THROUGH A VISION

I was once getting ready to minister at a service, and as I was making my way downstairs to the main auditorium, I suddenly had a vision of a hospital room. In the middle of the room, I saw what seemed like a small person in a hospital bed. I could not tell if it was an elderly person or a child, but the person I saw was bundled up in the sheets. I saw the top of the head and the color of the hair. I also saw an arm extended and a number of IVs inserted.

This vision came up a few times in very quick succession as I made my way to the front of the auditorium. I had come into the service midway through and was quickly handed the pulpit. Strangely, I felt no unction to talk about what I had seen, so I proceeded with the service.

About thirty minutes into the message, I suddenly saw the vision again. This time I felt a release to tell the congregation about it, so I did, trying to be as descriptive as possible. A man seated toward the back put his hand up and waved it excitedly. I motioned for him to come forward. He looked tired, and when I asked him about what I had seen, he told me that he and his family hadn't been back to church for a few months because his young son was sick in the hospital. The man had been at the hospital that evening with his wife when she said that since they were both tired and I was ministering, maybe it would be a good idea if he went to church. He had come to the service late, and within ten minutes of sitting down, I had shared about the vision.

The mercy of God had kept me from telling of the word of knowledge until its intended audience arrived. That word of knowledge encouraged and refreshed him. The next evening, the whole family, including their youngest son, showed up for the service. They had received permission from the doctors for the boy to come out. While his healing did not immediately manifest that evening, what that word of knowledge did was revive that family with the knowledge that God was well aware of where they were and the situation they faced. It was as if the Father put His arms around that family in a divine embrace.

JESUS HAD A WORD OF KNOWLEDGE THAT REACHED ONE WHO REACHED A REGION

"But He needed to go through Samaria."

JOHN 4:4

The unction of the Spirit can seem quite urgent sometimes, but the Holy Spirit never forces Himself on anyone. Demons force people, but the Holy Spirit never does. There is a level of yieldedness that we must develop toward the moving of the Spirit, and until we do, the manifestations of the Spirit will have little chance to operate through us. Since the Holy Spirit never forces anyone, it takes us willingly yielding for Him to flow through us.

The more we yield to the Spirit, the more tuned we get to the manifestations of the Spirit. This is a spiritual skill that we can intentionally develop. One prime way is by developing our prayer lives. In prayer, we learn and experience the flow of the Spirit. This is especially so when it comes to praying in the Spirit. Now, praying in the Spirit is not just praying in tongues. Praying in the Spirit is praying from the location of the Spirit. This often includes praying in tongues, but it can also include praying in our known tongue. However, praying in tongues is a quick way to enter the spirit realm because it literally bypasses the mind with all its hang-ups and opinions and allows us to have Spirit-to-spirit communication. The day of Pentecost, with its outpouring of the Spirit marked by the evidence of each individual disciple speaking in tongues, brought all believers into the realm of the miraculous. Tongues are the key.

The more we yield to the Spirit, the more tuned we get to the manifestations of the Spirit.

"The woman answered and said, 'I have no husband.' Jesus said to her, 'You have well said, 'I have no husband,' for you have had five husbands, and the one whom you now have is not your husband; in that you spoke truly.'"

JOHN 4:17-18

The reason Jesus *needed to go* to Samaria was to meet this one lady at the well. The background of the hostility between the Samaritans and the Jews reached far back into history. In the days of Joshua (Josh. 16-17), Samaria had been an allocated province to Ephraim and the half tribe of Manasseh. With the revolt of the northern tribes, they cut off most contact with the other tribes and had little to do with the temple in Jerusalem. They fell into idolatry and formed an unacceptable mixture of idolatry and Judaism. When a remnant returned from Babylon, they tried reestablishing a relationship with the main Jewish body again but were rebuffed. This resulted in bitter hatred and their opposition to what was held dear to all Jews: the rebuilding of the temple (Ezra 4:1-2; Neh. 4-6).

The Samaritans maintained that they were the true Jews and even had their own alternative temple. Things were so bad between the Samaritans and the Jews that the Rabbis would say, "To eat bread with Samaritans is like eating swine's flesh[2]."

All that is to say that the division between the Samaritans and the Jews was deep, wide, and old. That's why it took a specific urging of the Spirit to move Jesus into that region. It was not something any Jew would have done of his own accord.

The gifts of the Spirit do not just cross geographic and cultural boundaries, they can also bridge geographic and cultural differences. This was the setting for this miracle. It was a tense and awkward meeting—for the women, at least. But as we've said many times, the gifts will work outside of the church building, even with a skeptical and possibly hostile crowd.

To make matters even more challenging, the woman was not even a well-respected member of the Samaritan society. The reason she was drawing water at noon—the warmest

---

2   The Pulpit Commentary

part of the day in that desert region—was because she was an outcast. She did not want to be around when the other women drew water—or perhaps the other women did not want her around. Either way, the Samaritan woman was not a social loner by choice.

The manifestations of the Spirit always operate from a place of love. It is no mistake that following the great chapter on spiritual gifts, First Corinthians 12, the very next chapter is known as the great love chapter.

The manifestations of the Spirit always operate from a place of love.

The level of skill with which Jesus delivered the word of knowledge about this woman's numerous husbands was matched only by the loving way in which He asked her about them. He did not blurt out accusingly about her failed relationships; rather, He gently pointed out that the man she was with currently was one among many others she had lived with. He did not berate her for sinning and demand she renounce her lifestyle, but by a manifestation of the Spirit of truth and love, Jesus showed her that He knew her! This simple manifestation of the word of knowledge, coupled with love and wisdom, opened the door for a conversation that not only changed this woman but also elevated her to be an evangelistic voice in the region.

*"And many of the Samaritans of that city believed in
Him because of the word of the woman who testified,
'He told me all that I ever did.'"*

JOHN 4:39

One manifestation of the Spirit to touch the one individual can, in turn, touch a whole region.

> One manifestation of the Spirit to touch
> the one individual can, in turn, touch a
> whole region.

THE WORD OF WISDOM IN THE EVERYDAY

One thing I have noticed about the Father's love for us is
that He cares for the small details in our lives as much as
for what we would consider the greater events. Since I have
seen and accepted this truth, I have adjusted to accept that
the manifestations of the Spirit are not just for life-changing,
ministry-oriented events. If I will allow it, I can have these
manifestations in the everyday affairs of life as well. In fact,
I've found that the more I allow for the gifts in my daily life,
the sharper I become in the gifts in public ministry.

In the course of a year, I go on many international flights. I
adjust well to the travel, but it certainly helps when I get some
down time when I land. Once, when I landed after a long
international flight, I got into my rental car and drove myself

to the house my host had prepared for me. It was a huge place, and I was there all alone.

I unpacked quickly and immediately went to bed, waking up the next day at noon, just in time to head out to a lunch meeting. To my shock, after I had gotten dressed and ready to leave for lunch, I could not find my car keys. That horrid feeling you get when you lose something is only amplified when you are dealing with international time change and in a hurry.

I desperately rummaged through the bedroom and kitchen area but found nothing. I immediately had flashes in my mind of embarrassingly having to call my host and ask for a ride, having to call the rental company to pay for another key, or my schedule that day being changed because of this delay.

I had almost given up looking when I just casually said, "God, help me." Immediately, and to my surprise, I heard God reply, "It is in the trash bin in your room." I had not thought to look there and had completely forgotten that I had thrown out some receipts in my pocket the night before. Sure enough, when I looked in the trash among my receipts, there was the key.

You might be thinking, *Was the Holy Spirit given to help us find our keys?* The only way I could answer that is to tell you that the Holy Spirit was given for our benefit and the gifts for our profit. Our Father cares about the small, seemingly insignificant details of our lives.

The gifts are not just for public use in ministry. They are also for our benefit in life.

Chapter Three

FAITH

"…To another faith by the same Spirit…."
1 Corinthians 12:9

Paul started chapter 12 of First Corinthians telling us that we should not be ignorant of spiritual gifts. This could mean that we are totally unaware of them, but it could also mean that we just don't understand them enough to yield to the Holy Spirit when the unction is present for the gifts to manifest. It's sad, but I have noticed that the very thing we are told not to be ignorant of is exactly what many believers are ignorant of. Yet, ignorance of spiritual gifts is a choice, otherwise Paul would not have been inspired by the Holy Spirit to tell us not to be. I have found that there is an anointing to teach and reveal when we choose to obey God and "not be ignorant" of spiritual gifts.

We should not confuse the gift of faith with saving faith that brings someone into the family of God. It is supernatural in itself, but it is in a different category from the manifestation of faith listed here among the nine gifts of the Spirit. *Saving faith* is a gift from God to those who have yet to believe in Jesus, that they might believe in Him and receive the gift of eternal life. Saving faith comes as a result of hearing the gospel preached (Rom. 10:14). Faith for the gifts to manifest also comes by hearing because that is the only way faith legitimately comes (Rom. 10:17). That is really the reason for this book.

You can only have faith for what you hear about. By hearing/reading about the gifts, faith for them to manifest in your lives will come. That is what I am believing for you as we study together, that faith for these manifestations will increase in your lives.

So, there is saving faith that gets a person into the Kingdom of God, and then there is the faith that we live by as believers. In three parallel passages, believers are told that we are to walk by faith and not by sight (Hab. 2:4; Rom. 1:17; 2 Cor. 5:7). The life of a believer is supposed to be a life of faith—we call ourselves "believers," after all. The implication is that we believe something. We are not to be unbelieving believers. What do we believe? Well, we are supposed to believe everything that God promises us in His word. That is why faith to believe comes from hearing His Word.

Faith is so significant in the life of the believer that it is listed both as a fruit of the Spirit (Gal 5:22) as well as a gift of the Spirit in First Corinthians 12. The fruit of faith is for character. The gift of faith is for manifestation. As believers, the fruit of faith obeys what the Word says and is a sign of our salvation. The gift of special faith believes God in a way that compels Him to honor our word as He honors His own, miraculously bringing it to pass.

But the faith we are considering here is neither saving faith, the believer's faith, nor the fruit of faith. We are considering what we could call *the gift of special faith*.

Like all the other gifts of the Spirit, this manifestation is supernatural. While saving faith has a set expectation—salvation—the gift of faith deals in unexpected things. This gift of faith is a unique infusion from the Spirit, either to work a miracle or receive one.

> This gift of faith is a unique infusion from the Spirit, either to work a miracle or receive one.

You will find that many times there is a divine "pairing" that comes with the various gifts in operation. For example, the word of knowledge and the word of wisdom many times will come together. Diverse kinds of tongues and the interpretation of tongues are commanded to work together. The same can be said for the gift of faith and the working of miracles. These two gifts, although having some major differences, will oftentimes manifest together.

Although they both end with miraculous results, the gift of faith is distinct from the working of miracles in several ways:

- One receives a miracle. The other "works" a miracle.

- The operation of the gift of faith is more passive then active.
- The working of miracles is more active then passive.
- Although outwardly passive, the gift of faith unleashes a force that is irresistible and irreversible.

Unlike the previous two gifts, this is not listed as the "gift of a *word* of faith." Although words are *always* involved in the receiving and releasing of faith, that isn't how the Holy Spirit chooses to have this gift recorded for us. But in truth and definition, that is actually what it is. The gift of faith is a word from God's vast vocabulary of faith. God has a word of faith for every situation, and through the gift of faith, you could say, God gives us a word from His vast vocabulary for a specific situation.

The gift of faith is a set, specific faith targeted at specific situations. It is not a generic "God bless you" kind of faith; it is a specific "This is what will happen" kind of faith.

The gift of faith is a set, specific faith targeted at specific situations.

The spiritual gift of faith is a heavenly endowment to manifest the utterances of man. It is the undeniable functioning of

God in and through us without the involvement of human strength. It is a supernatural impartation of God's own divine faith to a human being. Since this manifestation is a portion of God's faith, it is as unlimited as He is.

You could say that the gift of faith is a sudden, supernatural ability to believe.

Of the many supernatural occurrences recorded for us in Scripture, those involving the gift of faith in operation have deep applications for us as believers, even if we are not operating in the gift of faith. This is because faith operates on principles, and even though the gift of faith is a unique function of faith, the principles we can mine from these accounts will still serve us as believers.

MOSES: THE GIFT OF FAITH SETS THE CAPTIVES FREE

The task of leading two million Hebrews with a slave mentality to freedom would require all kinds of supernatural assistance. But in Moses' case, not only did he have to lead the people, he also had to face the formidable Pharaoh and the Egyptian armies. The fact that Moses was successful with very limited cooperation from the Hebrews is a testament to what faith, patience, and the manifestations of the Spirit can accomplish.

The final thrust to free Israel from Pharaoh was a showdown of epic proportions. There is a parallel truth for us as New Testament believers. We are called, like Moses, to set the captives free. And just like Moses, we will need the arsenal of the Spirit to do so.

"So the Lord said to Moses: 'See, I have made you as God to Pharaoh, and Aaron your brother shall be your prophet.'"

EXODUS 7:1

I never fail to sense the magnitude of what God told Moses when I read this passage: "I have made you as God to Pharaoh."

God declared that Moses face Pharaoh as God. There was no way Moses could have lost because there is no way God can lose!

This is the prime purpose of the Holy Spirit's coming—the Holy Spirit in us causes us to be *as* God on the earth. I'm not saying that we *are* God, but that we are *like Him on the earth*. This was the only way we could have His presence in us and demonstrate His Life through us.

If this was so in the Old Testament, how much more so should it be in the New Testament?

How is the life of God demonstrated through us? By allowing the manifestations we have been studying. Every one of these gifts is an aspect of the power of God. We are not sent into this world unequipped.

"Then Moses and Aaron did so; just as the Lord commanded them, so they did."

EXODUS 7:6

Once when I was in prayer, through tongues and interpretation, the Lord showed me that the gift of faith is actually an expression of *unreasonable obedience*. You cannot obey unless you know what is expected of you in the first place. As F. F.

Bosworth said in the classic book on healing, *Christ the Healer*, "Faith begins where the will of God is known."

The Lord showed me that the gift of faith is actually an expression of unreasonable obedience.

As believers, the way we walk by faith is based on what the Word reveals to us. The gift of faith operates on the spur of a direct command to us. This may mean that a passage of scripture comes alive and jumps out to us or it may mean that the Spirit says something to us directly. Obviously, whatever the Spirit says will not contradict what the Word says since God will not contradict Himself, but it may not exactly be "chapter and verse." We can see Jesus doing this. There was no passage in scripture instructing Him to spit on the ground and stick the mud in the eyes of the blind man (John 9:6)—and thankfully, there is no passage instructing us to do likewise! Jesus was led to do that. He did not have a scriptural reference, but His actions agreed with God's will to heal (Exod. 15:26).

Faith and the will of God go hand in hand.

> *"When Pharaoh speaks to you, saying, 'Show a miracle for yourselves,' then you shall say to Aaron, 'Take your rod and cast it before Pharaoh, and let it become a serpent.'"*
>
> Exodus 7:9

Pharaoh demanding a miracle triggered what God had already instructed Moses to do. You could say that when God gave the order, the gift was put in place, but when Pharaoh demanded the miracle, the gift was activated. By the time the enemy demands a miracle of you, know that it has already been commanded and that you already carry what is necessary for that miracle. God, your Father, is never behind in the game. Let that strengthen you as you study these gifts. The gifts already given to you are more than enough to meet any challenge from the pharaohs in your path.

> *"So Moses and Aaron went in to Pharaoh, and they did so, just as the Lord commanded. And Aaron cast down his rod before Pharaoh and before his servants, and it became a serpent."*
>
> EXODUS 7:10

Really, when you ponder this, Moses would have been in a stressful scenario if he hadn't already had inside information on how the challenge would end. I don't suppose anyone likes being put on the spot, but Moses wasn't just on the spot. His life was on the line. I can only imagine that if he had failed to deliver the miracle as Pharaoh demanded, he would surely have been executed. This really was a case of do or die. Moses marching into Pharaoh's court and engaging in this exchange showed his great faith—the type of faith that was beyond that of the common believer. It was the gift of faith in action.

JOSHUA: THE GIFT OF FAITH STOPS TIME

"The Lord said to Joshua, 'Do not fear them, for I have delivered them into your hand; not a man of them shall stand before you.'"

JOSHUA 10:8

Personally, I think this is one of the greatest miracles recorded in the Bible.

Five Amorite kings decided to launch an attack on the Gibeonites as a punishment for their alliance with the Israelites. Since there was an alliance, Joshua was bound by honor to get involved in the conflict.

Faith always begins with the will of God. This is true for any category of faith, but with the gift of faith, it seems the will of God becomes more immediately known; there seems to be more of a process of study, meditation, and mind renewal that leads a common believer to knowing the will of God. Of course, I am not trying to imply that faith takes a long time to come. Faith comes the moment you agree with what you hear. But sometimes the process of hearing can take time.

I believe that when God spoke the end result, that was when He delivered the enemies into the hands of Joshua. You see, God speaks the end from the beginning. The battle had not even started, but God had already promised a victorious end. That is the essence of faith. Faith knows the result before the fight starts. So this was a faith fight for Joshua to begin with. Joshua entered the battle with the faith expected of any believer. But then, as the battle heated up and victory came into view, it seemed that they would not have enough daylight to finish the fight.

It is important that we end "fights." If we do not, then those same enemies will regroup and come at us again. But as the enemies were in retreat, the gift of faith came into manifestation.

> *"Joshua spoke to the Lord in the day when the Lord delivered up the Amorites before the children of Israel, and he said in the sight of Israel: 'Sun, stand still over Gibeon; and Moon, in the Valley of Aijalon.' So the sun stood still, and the moon stopped, till the people had revenge upon their enemies.' Is this not written in the Book of Jasher? So the sun stood still in the midst of heaven, and did not hasten to go down for about a whole day."*
> JOSHUA 10:12-13

Joshua had the heart of a finisher and the gift of faith allowed him to finish. What the enemy meant for evil and destruction, God, through the gift of faith, allowed Joshua to complete in total victory.

Joshua daring to command the sun and moon to stand still can only be understood as an act of inspired utterance. No man would otherwise dare dream of doing such a thing. The gift of faith causes you to say and act in ways that are out of the norm. Joshua did not ask that God do this. He simply stepped up, like Moses before Pharaoh, and acted as God in that situation. The gift of faith puts a person in the position and authority of God as His ambassador, speaking and acting on His behalf.

The gift of faith through Joshua, in this instance, had worldwide effects. We now know from science that the earth orbits around the sun. The rotation of the earth makes the sun appear to rise and set. So, it would appear that the earth stopped, not the sun. The gift of faith caused the earth to stop rotating. Consider what this could have caused: the oceans could have sent tidal waves sweeping across the earth. All the inhabitants of the earth could have been thrown into space. But none of that happened. The Lord accomplished this by suspending all the natural laws He created. The gift of faith goes beyond the natural laws of the universe.

The gift of faith caused the earth to stop rotating.

Outside of the gift of faith in operation, just on the basic principles of faith, this account says to me that when the enemy attempts to rob us of life, time, and opportunity, God can stop time. I would include lost and stolen opportunities, and even misused time, in this. God can turn back time to restore lost things to us, or He can stop time and allow for us to make corrections.

DANIEL: THE GIFT OF FAITH SHUTS THE LIONS' MOUTHS

This account of Daniel in the lions' den is a Sunday School favorite. Most kids, if they grew up in church, would have heard this at some point. But it was not included in the Bible just so that Sunday School teachers would have a story to tell. It was so that you and I could gain victory from it. While we can interpret this account literally—like all biblical accounts—there are also powerful principles for us to glean.

Like all Old Testament saints, Daniel was a man of powerful faith. By chapter six of the book of Daniel, he was a prisoner of war having been brought to Babylon from conquered Israel. Yet, his natural and spiritual characteristics caused promotion to come to him so that he had status and a say in the ruling of Babylon. His promotion in society caused jealousy from those around him.

Have you considered that God wants to bless you so much that those who do not know God will become jealous of you? You might think, *Well, I don't want people to be jealous of me.* But you see, when people do not know the source of your blessings or how to access them for themselves, jealousy is the natural response. You cannot stop people from becoming jealous, but you can live in such a way that is above reproach.

Those who were jealous of Daniel conspired against him to present false charges to the king. They cooked up a charge that by not bowing and praying to the king, Daniel was a lawless, disloyal subject. They elevated the king to the level of a god and created a cult of worship around him—just to kill Daniel!

Even though Daniel knew of their plans, he persisted in his relationship with God. He was not swayed. It was not the gifts of the Spirit through him, but his personal walk with God that kept him steady. Do not build your life on the gifts. Build your life developing a relationship with God through the Word and the Spirit. That is what will keep you strong and steady. The gifts manifest as the Spirit wills, but a steady walk with God will set you high daily.

It was this steadfastness that caused Daniel to persist in doing what he knew was right: refusing to bow to the king and continuing to pray to God. The king himself was bound by the law that he had been tricked into signing; he had no choice but to let Daniel be put into the lions' den. He regretted this foolishness so much that he had a sleepless night. The king was so desirous that Daniel be set free that he rushed to the den early the next morning to see if Daniel had survived.

> *"My God sent His angel and shut the lions' mouths, so that they have not hurt me, because I was found innocent before Him; and also, O king, I have done no wrong before you."*
>
> DANIEL 6:22

Unlike the king's sleepless night, Daniel was fully rested by the morning. He had gone into the den peacefully and was now emerging in the same state. The gift of supernatural faith causes you to sleep in the lions' den!

The gift of supernatural faith causes you to sleep in the lions' den!

This was a miracle, no doubt, but it was not the gift of the working of miracles; Daniel did no "work" to cause his miracle. It is a great example of the gift of faith in operation. When the gift of faith is flowing, you rest while angels work to shut lions' mouths.

You could say that the gift of faith always shuts the mouths of the lions.

One time, I was hosting a missions team of young adults from America in an Asian country. We were toward the end of the trip and finishing up with an evangelistic meeting in one of our village churches. It had been a three-night meeting, and this was the last night. The team was up front taking testimonies, and the crowd was enthusiastically praising God for each one. I was seated on the stage but the team was running the service.

As we came to the end of the testimonial part of the service, a lady in the fourth or fifth row suddenly jumped up started making loud, serpent-like hissing sounds, and began to slither-dance her way to the front. The pastors saw it and motioned the musicians to start singing, thinking to draw attention away from the lady. I moved toward the woman, planning to have her taken to the back where the team could minister to her while the service continued. While this was happening, the lady's serpent-like antics were drawing more and more attention. What happened next is mostly second-hand information from my team. I don't remember much of it myself.

I remember being indignant. It angered me that on the last night of what was otherwise a glorious series of meetings, the focus wasn't on God but rather on this hissing woman. That indignation rose on the inside of me like a tidal wave, and the next thing I'm told I did was jump off the stage and slap the woman upside the head in Jesus' name!

A hush fell over the congregation. The woman fell back on the floor and stayed there stiff as a board until we finished the service an hour and a half later. It then took her about an hour after that to come around. When she came to, she looked totally different. She was delivered. She didn't remember what had happened, but when told, she said that it had happened to her before. Her parents, who attended the meeting, also told the pastors that she had fallen into that type of trance before.

There had been many times that I have cast demons out of people before that service, but it was usually by much more subdued methods. Had it not been for the gift of faith in operation, I would never have had the boldness to jump off the stage and slap a woman—and in front of a crowd, no less!

Later, as I reflected more on what had happened, I saw how dangerous it could have been if I were not in the Spirit. A foreigner slapping a native could have caused riots in the streets. In the natural, I would have never thought or even felt right doing something like that.

Two years later, I was back in that same region, and after a service, that same lady came forward with her husband and a baby. She told me that they had always wanted a baby but had never been able to conceive. A few weeks after that service where she had been set free, she became pregnant. She had been delivered and healed!

I should say that it is important that we let the Spirit lead us into any of the manifestations of the gifts because it is "as the Spirit wills." I was not jumping off the stage and slapping people to be dramatic. When there is no prompting of the Spirit toward any of the gifts, then we do whatever it is we know in the Word to do. If there isn't a prophetic utterance that comes forth, then directing someone to a passage of scripture is just as effective. If the gifts of healings are not in operation, we can still lay hands on the sick as commanded in Mark 16.

When people try mimicking the manifestations of the Spirit without the leading of the Sprit, they make a mockery of the Spirit at best or open themselves up to familiar spirits at worst. Be led by the Holy Spirit. Jesus must be lifted up in all that we do!

The written Word of God, acted upon, can produce anything that the manifestations of the Spirit can do!

SHADRACH, MESHACH, AND ABED-NEGO ALSO HAD THE GIFT OF FAITH OPERATING THROUGH THEM

Of course, the stay in the lions' den was not the first time Daniel had been around the gift of faith in action. Daniel must have witnessed, or at least heard of, what had previously happened to Shadrach, Meshach, and Abed-Nego. Daniel was basically chief of staff for Nebuchadnezzar, one of the earlier kings that Daniel served in his long political career.

This story is another Sunday School favorite.

The similarities between the three Hebrew children's experience and Daniel's time in the lions' den is striking. In both situations, they were conspired against by those hostile to their faith, stood fast against the dictates of a ruler who demanded they compromise their beliefs, and then made a potentially life-ending decision for their faith.

> *"Shadrach, Meshach, and Abed-Nego answered and said to the king, 'O Nebuchadnezzar, we have no need to answer you in this matter.'"*
> DANIEL 3:16

When brought before Nebuchadnezzar for the high crime of not bowing to worship his image at the sound of the musical instruments, these young men showed a depth of wisdom that far surpassed their years. I have found that age and wisdom do not always arrive together; sadly, sometimes age comes alone.

Shadrach, Meshach, and Abed-Nego knew that the minds of Nebuchadnezzar and his advisors had been made up not at an intellectual level but at an emotional level because of a darkened heart. When logic meets emotions, emotions will win every time. Ours is a spiritual battle. I am thankful to God for the many capable and learned Christian intellectuals and apologists. I am always in awe when I listen to them and thankful that God has raised them up to influence others in their societal spheres. There is a place for the intelligent, articulated presentation of the things of God, but it is important to know that *the things of God are meant to be experienced by a hungry heart before they are understood by an inquiring mind.*

This is why we are told to "taste and see that the Lord is good" (Ps 34:8). There is a place of experiencing Him that surpasses our ability to understand. Our mind is limited. Our spiritual senses are not. On the day of Pentecost, in Acts 2, the disciples in the upper room experienced the outpouring of the Holy Spirit *before* they had an understanding of it.

As believers, we are *not* to *continue* having spiritual experiences without seeking clarification and confirmation from the Scriptures. Balance is not a bad word, but it will stifle us if we make our intellect the gauge for spiritual experiences. In fact, there are many spiritual experiences that our intellects will always have problems with. How does a Jewish carpenter's son being crucified on a Roman cross bring salvation to the world? Paul said it this way:

> "...But we preach Christ crucified, to the Jews a stumbling block and to the Greeks foolishness...Because the foolishness of God is wiser than men, and the weakness of God is stronger than men."
>
> 1 CORINTHIANS 1:23, 25

There are aspects of the spiritual realm that the human mind will never be able to comprehend. The same can be said for the study of the gifts of the Holy Spirit.

There are aspects of the spiritual realm that the human mind will never be able to comprehend. The same can be said for the study of the gifts of the Holy Spirit.

These gifts, as we see with the Corinthian church, were given to us by the Spirit of God before they were taught to us. This is because in the walk of the spirit, we are supposed to be in a place of continual learning and continual dependence upon the Holy Spirit. We learn as we grow, and we grow as we learn. This dislodges the human mind and the ego's need to know everything. We move in the things of the Spirit by faith and not by sight.

I am certain that if Shadrach, Meshach, and Abed-Nego had attempted an intellectual debate with their accusers, they would have talked themselves out of the realm of the miraculous.

What was it that emboldened them to defy the king? Faith in God.

"If that is the case, our God whom we serve is able to deliver us from the burning fiery furnace, and He will deliver us from your hand, O king. But if not, let it be known to you, O king, that we do not serve your gods, nor will we worship the gold image which you have set up."

DANIEL 3:17-18

The gift of faith operating through Shadrach, Meshach, and Abed-Nego did not reveal to them the details of their deliverance, but it did cause them to know that they were beyond the reach of the king's fury. Faith always knows the outcome, but seldom the details—and it usually doesn't care about those. Faith is an act. It does not need to know the outcome beforehand.

> *"And these three men, Shadrach, Meshach, and Abed-Nego, fell down bound into the midst of the burning fiery furnace. Then King Nebuchadnezzar was astonished; and he rose in haste and spoke, saying to his counselors, 'Did we not cast three men bound into the midst of the fire?' They answered and said to the king, 'True, O king.' 'Look!' he answered. 'I see four men loose, walking in the midst of the fire; and they are not hurt, and the form of the fourth is like the Son of God.'"*
>
> DANIEL 3:23-25

With the furnace heated seven times hotter than usual, the Hebrew children should have experienced the painful end the king wanted. But *the gift of faith always supersedes the natural!* The gift of faith is always in cooperation with Jesus Himself. Jesus is active with our faith just as our faith causes us to be active with Him. We might not always see Jesus at work with our physical eyes like Nebuchadnezzar when faith is in action, but Jesus always is.

JESUS: THE GIFT OF FAITH LAUNCHES PETER INTO THE DEEP

While we could say that every statement and action Jesus made was a statement of faith, there were also some clear instances where Jesus, as a man functioning under the anointing of the Holy Spirit, demonstrated moving in the gift of faith.

The gift of faith is a heavenly deposit of divine faith for a specific purpose at a specific time. No other occurrences of this gift we have studied or find in Scripture, continued manifesting in the same way repeatedly. We do not see Daniel continuing to have slumber parties in the lions' den, nor do we see Shadrach, Meshach, and Abed-Nego going into any more furnaces.

The gift of faith is a heavenly deposit of divine faith for a specific purpose at a specific time.

Simon was a fisherman who had just returned from an unsuccessful night of fishing. He and all who worked with him were back on shore cleaning their nets before heading home. Then Jesus came by and used Peter's boat to preach from. "When He had stopped speaking, He said to Simon, *'Launch out into the deep* and let down your *nets* for a catch'" (Luke 5:4).

The gift of faith came upon Jesus after He finished speaking. He turned His attention to Peter and issued a command that was contrary to the wisdom of the day. There was nothing in the natural to support Jesus' command. He just had a knowing that this would lead to success, restoration, and ultimately, the real call on Peter, James, and John's lives

With Jesus coming from a carpenter's background, it was actually Peter who was the professional authority in that situation. As a professional fisherman, he knew that during the day the fish would be too deep, beyond the reach of their nets. He could easily have dismissed Jesus' command. He had to set aside what he knew in the natural to follow Jesus. Faith always sidesteps the natural.

By the gift of faith in manifestation, Jesus boldly commanded that Peter go back and cast his nets where he had failed to catch anything the night before, in circumstances that were less favorable and with less energy. The gift of faith can turn a night of failure into a day of success.

> *"But Simon answered and said to Him, 'Master, we have toiled all night and caught nothing; nevertheless, at Your word I will let down the net.' And when they had done this, they caught a great number of fish, and their net was breaking."*
>
> LUKE 5:5-6

The gift of faith is *always* expressed by a command of faith. Jesus had told Peter to let down *nets*, but Peter only let down a singular net. God had bigger plans for this catch than could be contained in one net.

"So they signaled to their partners in the other boat to come and help them. And they came and filled both the boats, so that they began to sink."

LUKE 5:7

I love that another boat profited from this miracle. This is exactly what Paul said: "But the manifestation of the Spirit is given *to each one for the profit of all*" (1 Cor. 12:7). We are all robbed when we do not allow for the gifts to manifest in our lives. Through the gifts, God intends to fill our boats *and* those of other people as well!

Chapter Four

HEALINGS

"...To another gifts of healings by the same Spirit."
1 Corinthians 12:9

The world so desperately needs all the manifestations of the Spirit but perhaps none more so than the gifts of healings. The world as a whole—those in the Church included—are facing more physical challenges than ever. Yet, the Word and the Spirit of God have not changed. The solution remains the same. Our God is a healing God, and the healing of the total man remains the children's bread (Matt. 15:26).

> The world so desperately needs all the manifestations of the Spirit but perhaps none more so than the gifts of healings.

Our Father's great desire for our total healing may be why this gift is one of two manifestations listed in the plural form:

the *gifts* of *healings* (the other is diverse kinds of tongues, which we will study later). There is great variation to these healing gifts in operation.

The plurality of this operation stems from the fact that it is "by His *stripes*" that we are healed (Isa. 53:5). The multiple stripes of Jesus resulted in the multiple forms of our complete healing.

We should remember that because God, our Father, created us as spirit, soul, and body (1 Thess. 5:23) to be complete, that's how He sees us—in three parts. No part is more important than the other. So we could say that since our Father is good to us and wants us whole, He must also, out of necessity, provide healing for us spirit, soul, and body. There is complete healing for the total man. That is part of the reason why the gifts of healings are plural.

I suppose that no one believer can have all the gifts of healings flowing through him or her at any one time. You can easily see that if anyone did, they would quickly be seen by the world as God Himself. The healing of the physical body is a tangible sign both to the believer and the unbeliever of the supernatural in action.

The gifts of healings supernaturally alleviate or restore a body that has been hurt or diseased. Healing from God is not always immediate. Miracles, which we will study later, usually are.

While I do not doubt that God is behind the advancement of the medical help available in our modern age, we should not confuse that with the gifts of healings. The former is the harnessing of the natural to aid the body in healing. The latter is the suspending and reversal of the natural by the supernatural. Some in the past have taken the extreme position that the medical profession is not necessary if one is to believe God. They seem to have forgotten that God clearly had no issues with Luke being a medical doctor. He was the human scribe of both a gospel and the Acts, and at no point was he ever told to recant his medical training.

HEALING AT EVERY TURN

Before we look at the manifestation of the gifts of healings in a little more depth, I should let you know that there are a variety of ways outside of the gifts that God offers healing. Again, this points to the truth that God is very desirous for us to receive healing. He offers us healing at every turn. We are never left waiting for the gifts to manifest before we can receive healing. Nor should we ever be stuck waiting for someone who moves in the gifts of healings to come through our town. Obviously, I believe in the manifestations of the Spirit, and I believe in men and women anointed by God who move in the gifts. But those are both possible avenues of healing, not the only ones.

1) Pray and Ask for Yourself

> "Is anyone among you suffering? Let him pray. Is anyone cheerful? Let him sing psalms."
>
> JAMES 5:13

We have this glorious invitation to go directly to Him if we are suffering in any way. Who can argue that any form of sickness is not suffering? There is an aspect of this that is so precious because it is so personal. We can go directly to our Father!

There is something about all these manifestations of the Spirit that personalizes our experience with God. They make His presence and power expand beyond the throne room and into our living room. If one is suffering, as James says, it is then a given that if the person prayed, he or she would ask that the suffering be alleviated. The person would ask for healing. Asking is worthless unless we are expecting an answer. This expectation is called faith.

There is something about all these manifestations of the Spirit that personalizes our experience with God. They make His presence and power expand beyond the throne room and into our living room.

Asking God implies the following:

- We believe that what we are asking for is available from God.
- We believe that God is willing to give our request to us. Why else would He invite us to ask?

So, as James says: PRAY!

2) The Laying on of Hands

The laying on of hands is not just another tradition in the Church; it's a command from God (Mark 16:17) and an ordinance in the Church (Heb. 6:2). The command was given to *all* believers. This makes any believer a possible conduit of the healing power of God. It was apparently important enough that Jesus gave those instructions as part of His last words before His ascension. So, if you need healing, have hands laid on you by believing believers.

3) The Spoken Word of Faith

James 5 is a rather isolated verse when it comes to healing. Prayer is seldom prescribed in the Word concerning healing. Healing, as quoted in Matthew's gospel (Matt. 8:16-17) and prophesied by Isaiah (53:4), was a promised fact that we simply needed to reach out and take. You do not have to pray and ask for what God has already promised you. Just take it! One way you take what God has promised you is by simply saying, in faith, what God has already said. When we say what God says, the power of God's words become the power of ours. So, if you need healing, say what God says.

A few years ago, I developed an ache in my left toe that just would not go away. It started by just being tender to the touch, but it quickly developed to where it became so sore that I could not fully stand on it. I was keeping such a busy ministry schedule that I did not even think enough of it to pray. I just kept thinking that maybe I had been standing too long and need to rest more. The pain crept into my life and just stayed there. That's how the enemy tries to sneak into so many areas of our lives—quietly and slowly.

Finally, I went to the doctor's office to have my toe looked at, and after all the tests were completed, I was surprised when they told me I had early onset arthritis. Part of what surprised me was that I had ministered to people with arthritis and seen them instantly set free. The things of God come to us only when we are intentionally open to receiving them, otherwise we miss out. Now, I understand that we cannot be intentional about *all* that God wants for us because it's so far beyond our imagination, but we must try to always be in a receptive frame of mind to the good that our Father intends for us.

As soon as I got home from the doctor's office, I went into my bedroom and sat on the edge of my bed. I held my left foot with both hands, took authority over the swelling and pain, and commanded the arthritis to depart from me. I prayed and worshiped in tongues for about fifteen minutes as I walked around the room, and by the end of that period, the pain and swelling had left my toe completely. And it has never come back!

There is power in taking what belongs to us.

4) Prayer Cloths and Anointing Oil: Extensions of the Anointing

"Now God worked unusual miracles by the hands of Paul, so that even handkerchiefs or aprons were brought from his body to the sick, and the diseases left them and the evil spirits went out of them."

ACTS 19:11-12

"Is anyone among you sick? Let him call for the elders of the church, and let them pray over him, anointing him with oil in the name of the Lord."

JAMES 5:14

God is so eager to reach us that any time we make a move toward Him, He leaps toward us. The anointing is a tangible, spiritual substance. Like anything tangible, it has the potential of being put "on" something. The power in the prayer cloths from Paul's hands was not in the cloth itself but in the anointing on Paul and the faith of the people who received the cloths. The anointing oil was just oil until it was applied in faith. Faith activates the anointing. Faith activates anything God has for us. Prayer cloths and anointing oil are both variations of the laying on of hands. Where hands cannot be laid, cloths and oils can be utilized instead.

When the Lord first started leading me to lay hands on cloths, I had already been laying hands on the sick for many years. One day He said to me, "I want to teach you how the anointing can be extended." That helped me understand what the prayer cloths represented. They were simply extensions of the anointing.

After a service where the people had yielded to the Spirit and many had fallen on the floor, hit by holy laughter, two ladies came up to me with a big stack of handkerchiefs. They told me that they had a street evangelism outreach and would regularly go downtown to witness and minister to addicts and homeless people. They asked that I lay hands on the cloths they brought in case they were led to give them away. I gladly did so and didn't think any more of it.

About two weeks later, one of the ladies contacted the office on social media and shared that when she went out witnessing one evening, she came across a young man—a recovering addict. After they shared the good news of the gospel with him and laid hands on him, they handed him one of the prayer cloths. They told him that the cloths had been prayed for and that the anointing of God on them would aid in his recovery.

As he held the cloth in his hands, listening to them, they said he started swaying. He looked like he was trying to concentrate on what they were saying, but soon he fell over on the sidewalk and started to belly laugh in the Spirit. When he got up, he said the desire for drugs was not on him anymore. The manifestation he experienced on the sidewalk was the same manifestation we had in the service the night the cloths were prayed over. The anointing can travel out of the sanctuary of the church in prayer cloths to bring healing and deliverance.

The gifts of healings are intertwined with, and sometimes almost indistinguishable from, the operation of the other gifts. The gifts of healings can be tagged on and operate through any one of the other gifts. What is important for us is not to just grasp an intellectual, textbook definition but to understand the gifts themselves. Our purpose in studying them should stir us to "covet earnestly the best gifts" (1 Cor. 12:31) and to hunger to yield ourselves to the Holy Spirit. In yielding to the Holy Spirit, all these manifestations will function through us.

As believers, we have the anointing in us and all nine gifts of the Spirit are aspects of that anointing. So, when we flow and yield to the anointing, the gifts follow easily.

JESUS MOVED IN THE GIFTS OF HEALINGS

"And when John had heard in prison about the works of Christ, he sent two of his disciples and said to Him, 'Are You the Coming One, or do we look for another?' Jesus answered and said to them, 'Go and tell John the things which you hear and see: The blind see and the lame walk; the lepers are cleansed and the deaf hear; the dead are raised up and the poor have the gospel preached to them.'"

MATTHEW 11:2-5

Jesus is the most consistent example we have in Scripture of the gifts of healings in operation. There was healing happening with the ministry of Jesus at every turn. Besides His love for people and wanting to see them set free, there was a greater reason why Jesus was such a healer.

Jesus is the most consistent example we have in Scripture of the gifts of healings in operation.

He used physical healings as a means to establish His identity and the proclamation of the Kingdom. It is telling that when John the Baptist asked for a confirmation of Jesus' identity, it was the physical healings that Jesus submitted as proof. This tells us the importance of healing in the ministry of Jesus. If John the Baptist, who had a revelation of Jesus as the

Lamb of God that takes away the sin of the world (John 1:29), needed proof of Jesus' identity, how much more would those that did not have a revelation of Jesus need a sign? Healing is not just for the human body; it is for the establishment of the Kingdom rule.

A LEPER CLEANSED

"Now a leper came to Him, imploring Him, kneeling down to Him and saying to Him, 'If You are willing, You can make me clean.' Then Jesus, moved with compassion, stretched out His hand and touched him, and said to him, 'I am willing; be cleansed.' As soon as He had spoken, immediately the leprosy left him, and he was cleansed."

MARK 1:40-42

In the time of Jesus, leprosy was a major life threat—socially and religiously. Socially, lepers were isolated for fear of infecting the greater population. Since they had no medical cure available, once leprosy struck, the lepers were carted off to an isolated colony. There was restricted access from relatives and nearly no allowance for the lepers to interact with community. If lepers were to see people approaching, they had to yell out "unclean" so that pedestrians would know to stay clear. Lepers could be stoned if they tried approaching a populated area unannounced.

Religiously, leprosy was seen as a curse or judgment from God. While leprosy certainly is not a blessing, the idea that God Himself cursed people with leprosy made lepers untouchable.

So, when we read the accounts of Jesus healing lepers, He was not just reversing a physical ailment, but Jesus was literally restoring a life back to that individual. Prophetically, this is a picture of the completeness that only the ministry of Jesus can bring.

This leper knew Jesus *could* heal, but he did not know if Jesus *would* heal. In the Old Testament, lepers were so despised that if a priest came in contact with one, the priest was immediately pronounced unclean. But in the New Testament, when the leper came into the presence of Jesus, our High Priest, the leper was made clean.

This leper knew Jesus *could* heal, but he did not know if Jesus *would* heal.

What activated the Father's manifestation of healings? Compassion! This is God's heart toward the world. Compassion is not to be confused with sympathy. Compassion is a heavenly force that can usher in the healing power of God. Sympathy is a human emotion, a counterfeit to heavenly compassion, that does little to produce a heavenly result.

This particular healing of the leper was administered through the laying on of hands and a command of faith. This is not a formula because we do not see this as the standard way that Jesus ministered healing. There is no standard way that Jesus ministered healing, which would mean that there was an internal leading that Jesus followed. The leading of the Spirit is vital to the manifestation of the gifts. Since the gifts are Holy Spirit given, it would make sense that they must also be Holy Spirit led.

How was Jesus led to minister in such diverse ways?

> *"Then Jesus answered and said to them, 'Most assuredly, I say to you, the Son can do nothing of Himself, but what He sees the Father do; for whatever He does, the Son also does in like manner.'"*
> JOHN 5:19

Jesus did what he "saw" the Father doing. How and when did Jesus see the Father lay hands on a leper?

Seeing into the realm of the Spirit is a function of the spirit man. Paul prayed that the eyes of our understanding be enlightened (Eph. 1:18). Our spirit man has the capacity to have enlightened sight, seeing into the realm of the spirit where all the illusions of the physical realm are stripped away. It was in this realm that Jesus saw the Father.

Is the Father laying hands on lepers in heaven? In a sense, I believe what Jesus saw was an expression of what the Father desired. He desired to lay hands on the leper, and He did so through the hands of Jesus. The Father has no hands on the earth outside of the hands available in the Body of Christ. God wills to use your hands, your legs, your mouth, every part of you for His service!

His hands, our hands. His words, our words. They become one when we yield to the Spirit. The manifestations of the Spirit must be yielded to by an act of our free will.

That Paul prayed for our enlightened sight means that not all sight is enlightened. Since enlightened sight sees clearly into the spirit realm, unenlightened sight, then, must be sight that does not see into the reality of the spirit realm.

Enlightened sight is a result of a deeper life in the things of God. This includes developing a personal prayer life, taking time to contemplate and mediate on the Word of God, and learning to recognize and honor the person of the Holy Spirit.

Enlightened sight is a result of a deeper life in the things of God.

Seeing Him is how we become like Him.

> *"Beloved, now we are children of God; and it has not yet been revealed what we shall be, but we know that when He is revealed, we shall be like Him, for we shall see Him as He is."*
>
> 1 JOHN 3:2

TEN MORE LEPERS CLEANSED

> *"Then as He entered a certain village, there met Him ten men who were lepers, who stood afar off. And they*

lifted up their voices and said, 'Jesus, Master, have mercy on us!' So when He saw them, He said to them, 'Go, show yourselves to the priests.' And so it was that as they went, they were cleansed."

LUKE 17:12-14

Another time, a group of ten lepers came seeking Jesus. As they stood far off, they cried out for mercy. They did not cry out for physical healing, but the mercy of God is the reason for all our physical healings. How powerful a cry for mercy is to God! The Father's heart is all mercy toward us. In calling for mercy, they received everything that mercy could give.

Jesus' response was an unusual one. He instructed them to go show themselves to the priest because the temple priests were the ones tasked with determining what was clean or unclean. No leper would bother making that trip to see the priest because there was never any reversal once the dreaded disease took root. Unlike the previous account of leprosy being healed, this time, Jesus did not lay hands on anyone; instead He had them walk out their healing. It says that "as they went" they were cleansed.

Gifts of healings always come with an instruction or action. It might be as simple as laying hands on someone, speaking a command of faith, or even laying hands on a cloth to be sent to the afflicted. Healing must be acted upon; it must be appropriated. It must be received in faith. In their going, the lepers were cleansed of the disease. There is a "going" in order to receive from Jesus. Sometimes the going is having done all to stand, stand therefore (Eph. 6:13). Going is our cooperation in response to the gifts of healings.

Gifts of healings always come with an instruction or action.

The command to show themselves to the priest was a command of the gift of faith in action, and it resulted in the gifts of healings cleansing the lepers. One of them—a Samaritan—when he saw he was healed, returned and glorified God, falling on his face and giving Him thanks.

> *"So Jesus answered and said, 'Were there not ten cleansed? But where are the nine? Were there not any found who returned to give glory to God except this foreigner?' And He said to him, 'Arise, go your way. Your faith has made you well.'"*
>
> Luke 17:17-19

One aspect of leprosy is that it permanently disfigures its victims by swelling, bumps, and lumps. Also, because of the nerve damage, lepers usually had scabs from cuts that they never even felt. You can imagine that in wandering that desert environment, they looked every bit like Hollywood's version of the mummy.

While the ten went toward the priest, they were miraculously cleansed. One of those men, a Samaritan, came back to thank and worship Jesus. Jesus then made an interesting proclamation over him: "Arise, go your way. Your faith has made you *well*" (Luke 17:19). The King James version translates *well* as *whole* from the Greek word *sozo* (Strong's 4982). Vine's Expository Dictionary agrees with this, saying that *sozo* means "to make whole."

This is vastly different from what happened to the original group of ten as they made their way to the priest. In verse 14, it simply tells us that they were "cleansed." The Greek word used here is *katharizo* (Strong's 2511), which simply means "to make clean."

It is one thing to be cleansed of leprosy but a totally different thing to be made whole and restored. While nine were set free from leprosy but still scarred, this Samaritan had his disfigurations reversed.

The Samaritan's appreciation of what Jesus and the healing anointing did in his life caused the gifts of healings to move into a further manifestation. This is an example of the variation of the gifts, and why there are *gifts of healings* (plural).. It was one operation of the spiritual gifts to cleanse leprosy, but it is another operation of spiritual gifts to restore disfigurations.

> The power of thankfulness opens us up to appreciate the things that are right, taking our attention away from the things that are wrong.

The power of thankfulness opens us up to appreciate the things that are right, taking our attention away from the things that are wrong. Whatever we give our attention to is magnified, and whatever we magnify will automatically overshadow everything else. When this Samaritan worshipped Jesus for his cleansing, he opened himself up for more.

Thank and worship God for the things that are right in your life. Yes, there is a place to believe Him to fix the negatives in your life, but if that's all you do, your concentration is on the wrong thing. If you are believing for healing, include praising and worshipping God for what is right with you daily.

DELIVERANCE FROM DEMONS IS PART OF THE FUNCTION OF THE GIFTS OF HEALINGS

"How God anointed Jesus of Nazareth with the Holy Spirit and with power, who went about doing good and healing all who were oppressed by the devil, for God was with Him."

ACTS 10:38

You could rightly say that Satan is the author of all sickness, but he is not always the *direct* author. For example, I've known of people who have unhealthy eating habits. If they get sick because of how they eat, it would not be Satan directly causing that sickness. Yet, he will definitely try to take advantage of an opportunity offered to him. The solution, in that case, would not be just binding the devil but the people changing... what they eat as well.

There is an aspect of healing that we must see holistically. I've had people ask me if they could go to heaven if they smoked cigarettes. I replied that it really depended on how many they smoked; if they smoked a lot, they might go to heaven a whole lot quicker than they were thinking!

On the other hand, we also fall into a ditch if we totally ignore demonic activity. It's a mistake to only give medical and emotional problems a name tag and then try to medicate them. You cannot medicate demons. As I have said, I believe in doctors and medicine if they're needed. But it would be a mistake as believers if that's all we ever do.

You see, healings started occurring very quickly in the Gospels during Jesus' ministry, as with the lepers, but then there were also times where demonic activity was specifically named as the cause of the problem.

> *"Then one was brought to Him who was demon-possessed, blind and mute; and He healed him, so that the blind and mute man both spoke and saw."*
>
> MATTHEW 12:22

Demons were responsible for this man being blind and mute. We don't see every blind and mute person in the Bible recorded this way, but we do with him. This man's deliverance came about as a result of his healing. His healing and deliverance were not separate events. They happened simultaneously.

> *"As they went out, behold, they brought to Him a man, mute and demon-possessed. And when the demon was cast out, the mute spoke...."*
>
> MATTHEW 9:32-33

Again, here was a mute, demon-possessed man, who received healing and deliverance together. The plurality of the gifts of healings includes deliverance from demons.

Deliverance is just a different administration, a diversity of the gifts of healings.

Many times when ministering, I will sense the anointing in waves. When I do, it almost always seems to build with each new wave coming into the room. This is what I sensed one night as I ministered at the end of a series of meetings.

The stage I stood on was raised quite high, and I could see all the way to the back of the auditorium. It was a large building, and the altars were packed with people who had come forward to receive healing. I had not sensed to lay hands on them individually. I had been led to have anyone seeking healing come down, and then I was to speak over them collectively.

As the people were standing down front, praising God and starting to act out their healings, my attention was drawn to the right side in the back of the hall. It seemed like the people standing there were quickly clearing a space around a man.

I stood on my toes to see a little clearer and saw that there was a man who had taken one of the folded chairs and was swinging it wildly around himself. The moment I looked in his direction, he looked up, locked eyes with me, and shook a fist. I couldn't hear him all the way through the hall because of the sound of everyone else praising and worshipping, but I could see him seemingly yelling at me. He literally looked like he was spitting and cursing.

I paused to check in my heart and ask what the Lord would have me do. Just then, I sensed another wave of the anointing coming into the room. As that wave came, I waved my hands in his direction and mouthed the word *peace*. It was not loud enough for the microphone to pick up, but the moment

I did, I saw him fall over at the back of the hall as that wave of the anointing hit him. After the service, as I was walking out, I saw that he was still on the floor exactly where he had fallen over.

The next day, the committee that had helped organize the conference came over to have a debriefing meeting. One of them excitedly told me that the man from the night before worked for him and had snuck into the meeting late. As a young child, his parents had brought him to a heathen temple and dedicated him to one of the idols there. A week later, as a child of about three, his left foot suddenly turned inward toward his right foot, and he hadn't walked normally since. But after the service the night before and after he came to from being hit by the anointing, his left foot was straightened out. No one even prayed for his healing, but when he was delivered from those demons, he was also delivered from what they caused in his body.

The same anointing, the same gifts of healings, that can bring physical healing can also bring deliverance.

The same anointing, the same gifts of healings, that can bring physical healing can also bring deliverance. And many times, deliverance will bring physical healing.

FLOWING IN THE GIFTS OF HEALINGS

The first step to flowing in any of the spiritual manifestations, besides hungering for them, is to do whatever you see the Word says. You do not need the gifts of healings to lay hands on the sick. Mark 16 tells you to lay hands on the sick. As you obey the Word in what you see, the Spirit will lead you into all else—this includes the manifestations of the Spirit. I have noticed that some people who have been trained to yield to the gifts of healings can have more success in ministering healing to one type of sickness than others. This is because they may only have one of the multiple gifts of healings for a certain sickness. For example, I know of some ministers who have greater success ministering to people with bad backs. I know of others who have a ministry where growths and tumors melt away when they pray.

The gifts of healings are a diverse and powerful operation of the Spirit!

EPILOGUE: OUR SOUL NEEDS HEALING

While I personally have never heard of the gifts of healings taught from the angle of God wanting to heal our souls—that is our wills, emotions, intellects, memories, and imaginations—I have come to see from studying Scripture and the leading of the Spirit that God's ability and willingness to heal must include our souls. Since He wills for our souls to be healed, then by extension, an aspect of the gifts of healings must include healing for the soul.

"The Spirit of the Lord is upon Me, because He has anointed Me...He has sent Me to heal the brokenhearted."

LUKE 4:18

Again, I contend that God wants all parts of us healed and whole. And since the gifts of healings are an expression of God's heart, then they must also, of necessity, be able to bring healing and restoration to all parts of man, spirit, soul, and body.

The cross of Calvary made it possible for the spirit of man to be recreated, the soul of man to be renewed, and the body of man to be healed.

The cross of Calvary made it possible for the spirit of man to be recreated, the soul of man to be renewed, and the body of man to be healed.

The cross of Calvary provides healing for the total man!

Like any other area where there is divine truth, the enemy has tried to muddy these waters of emotional healing up as well. It is unscriptural for believers to take years on end to nurse and continually rehearse past hurts and grievances to "counselors."

No one can heal from a hurt that they choose to hold onto. Rehearsing and repeating the past is a sure way to never heal from anything. I am not talking about suppressing any hurts.

There are times to talk about things in the past that have happened, but that should be to others who can provide the right scriptural and emotional counsel so that forgiveness and wholeness can come.

Forgiveness is a command to us. Walking in love is a command to us.

We act on both as a choice and not a feeling.

However, I do also recognize that hurts to the soul are as real as hurts to the body, and just as God wants our bodies well, He also wants our souls to be whole.

Even in the Old Testament, we see pictures of God wanting to heal His people in places beyond the physical body.

> *"The Lord is near to the brokenhearted and saves those who are crushed in spirit."*
> PSALM 34:18 NIV

> *"He heals the brokenhearted and binds up their wounds."*
> PSALM 147:3

In a real way, as doctors are now telling us, a person's mental and emotional health dictates their physical well-being. Or as it says in Proverbs 17:22: "A merry heart does good, like medicine, but a broken spirit dries the bones."

This would make scriptural sense because we are created as a tripartite being, and God did not intend for any of our individual parts to function independently of each other.

I had the opportunity a few years ago to minister at a youth and young adults retreat. During one of the evening services,

I sensed the healing anointing come into the room. As we yielded to that anointing, I called out a few individuals by way of words of knowledge and laid hands on them. There were quite a few instantaneous healings.

Just when I thought we were almost at the end of the service, I heard the Spirit say, "There is healing for the broken-hearted. Tonight, I want to teach you how I will heal them."

I felt restrained from repeating this to the congregation, and so I just waited on the Spirit for further instructions. In a little while, I heard the Lord tell me to, "Start declaring my love over the people." So, I started speaking about God's love for us. I did not teach or preach about it; I simply declared it over the people. I said things like, "He loved us before we first loved Him." "God loves us with an everlasting love." "What great love the Father has lavished on us."

I continued speaking over the people collectively and soon there were people crying and sobbing throughout the hall. There was even a young lady at the back of the room who screamed as she was delivered from demons.

I continued ministering along those lines until I sensed the anointing lift.

The next afternoon, a young lady put her hand up as the service was being handed back to me. She said she wanted to give a testimony and shared a heart-wrenching story of how she had been abused and abandoned as a child, and as an older teen, had been cutting herself. But after the service the night before, she felt the weight of sadness and depression lift off her. As she shared that, about six other young people got up to share almost the same thing. They had been lifted from sadness, depression, and cutting. The sense of dread was broken over them. By the time the retreat ended, I had nearly twenty people come tell me they had been delivered from brokenness and suicidal depression.

I have since had quite a few more meetings where the Spirit has led me to minister along those lines.

> *"Do not be conformed to this world, but be trans-formed by the renewal of your mind, that by testing you may discern what is the will of God, what is good and acceptable and perfect."*
>
> ROMANS 12:2 ESV

Like with anything else we receive from the Lord, we must maintain it; we still live in a fallen earth with a fallen environment. The way we maintain healing from a hurt soul is to keep our minds renewed with the Word of God.

Our thoughts determine our feelings, and our feelings determine our actions.

When we keep our minds on what God's Word says about us, our renewed minds will strengthen us against any hurts or recurrences of hurts.

Chapter Five

THE WORKING OF MIRACLES

"…To another the working of miracles…."
1 Corinthians 12:10

The working of miracles is the divine stepping into the natural. Miracles are a sovereign act of the Spirit of God; a miracle with a natural explanation cannot be a miracle.

The working of miracles is the divine stepping into the natural.

The working of miracles is a gift that manifests the ability of God to intervene, supersede, or alter natural law. At their source, miracles are purely divine, but they always flow through natural means. So rather than create water out of nothing for the flood of Noah's day, God used water from natural rain and from the oceans rising (Gen. 7:11). The gift of the working of miracles *always* works through human and natural means. There are occurrences recorded in the Bible that are miraculous but did not come through human involvement—such as Moses' burning bush. These are miracles, just not the gift of the working of miracles.

Miracles are not the doing away of the natural, but rather, the enlarging or downsizing of the natural.

This gift was in manifestation much more in the Old Testament than the New Testament. This was because the Old Testament revealed the power of God while the New Testament revealed the compassion of the Father.

THE WORKING OF MIRACLES BRINGS SUPERNATURAL SUPPLY

"Then the Lord said to Moses, 'Behold, I will rain bread from heaven for you. And the people shall go out and gather a certain quota every day, that I may test them, whether they will walk in My law or not.'"

EXODUS 16:4

Among other things, this miracle teaches us that there can be a daily reliance on God for a fresh supply. I love that God wants to be in our daily lives. He isn't just God of the "big" miracle. He is the God of the daily "smaller" miracles. An understanding of miracles removes our need to hoard anything and puts us in a place of continual expectation. This same principle is repeated in what we know as the Lord's prayer. "Give us this day our daily bread" (Matt. 6:11).

When we grasp the significance of the gift of working miracles, it puts an excitement in every morning because it's yet another opportunity to have a fresh delivery of heavenly manna. Neither "hand to mouth" nor "laid up wealth" is the plan of God for us. It is daily willingness to let yesterday's manna go and to expect from heaven. Of course, this is not to say that we must not have any material possessions, but rather, that our trust is not in what we can gather in our hands. Our trust is to be in what God will bring *to* our hands. This is the posture that sets the stage for the gift of the working of miracles.

Manna from heaven was not the only time God, through the cooperation of Moses, brought miraculous supply. God also brought water from a rock.

> *"Behold, I will stand before you there on the rock in Horeb; and you shall strike the rock, and water will come out of it, that the people may drink.' And Moses did so in the sight of the elders of Israel."*
>
> EXODUS 17:6

Having journeyed deep into the desert and now facing opposition from the armies of Amalak and a drought, the children of Israel were beginning to murmur against Moses. Reaching a fever pitch, some were even thinking of stoning him. But through the gift of the working of miracles, Moses struck the rock and water came forth.

Typically with God, every act, every utterance, every miracle speaks at multiple levels. While the children of Israel rightly saw this miracle as a means to end their thirst, God used this event to speak prophetically of the crucifixion of the coming Christ. Jesus was to be the Rock that was struck and had living water poured forth from it (John 19:34). Jesus was to be sacrificed once and for all (Heb. 6:6).

Moses clearly did not see the significance himself because he made some changes to God's plan the next time water from a rock was called for.

> *"Then Moses lifted his hand and struck the rock twice with his rod; and water came out abundantly, and the congregation and their animals drank. Then the Lord spoke to Moses and Aaron, 'Because you did not believe Me, to hallow Me in the eyes of the children of Israel, therefore you shall not bring this assembly into the land which I have given them.'"*
>
> Numbers 20:11-12

Moses, out of anger and frustration with the people, struck the rock twice instead of once as commanded. God forbade Moses and Aaron from entering the promised land, not because He was petty, but because, symbolically, those who entered the Promise Land must be those who believed that Jesus, the Rock, was struck once and for all.

The gifts of the Spirit, specifically the working of miracles in this situation, were used by God to demonstrate His power, provide for the children of Israel, and speak to us today through the Old Testament type of Rock. There truly are diverse administrations with the ways of God.

The fact was that Moses was commanded to strike the rock once, but he did it twice. He disobeyed God and nearly messed up an important prophetic picture of Jesus, but the miracle still happened. The people drank of the water and could enter the Promise Land, but Moses, who was used in the working of that miracle, could not. Miracles can happen independently of the minister's current walk with God. *Spiritual gifts are independent of spiritual growth.* The church in Corinth was another example of this. They had an abundance of every spiritual manifestation but also were overrun with sin and division. These gifts of the Spirit are all given from God's throne of grace and mercy.

I think the life of Samson, with all his flaws and heartache, proves this without a doubt. Samson had the miraculous flowing through every part of his life. From the angelic announcement of his birth to his long hair and supernatural strength, Samson's life was a sign and wonder from the start. Yet, the Bible records that he had an impetuous streak. He was prone to rowdiness and forsook his religious vows with alcohol and women. And and then there was Delilah.

I am always thankful that God chose to record flawed characters in the Bible as people He was still able to move through by His Spirit. It gives hope to all of us. Outside of Jesus, every character in the Bible was flawed. There was not a perfect one among them. But it did not stop the Spirit from giving out His gifts to them, and it did not stop the gifts from manifesting through them. Our flaws are not greater than the Spirit's flow!

 Outside of Jesus, every character in the Bible was flawed. There was not a perfect one among them. But it did not stop the Spirit from giving out His gifts to them.

The working of miracles is a coming together of human involvement to do the "working," and God the providing of the "miracle."

In Elijah's ministry, we see the working of miracles once again providing for material needs—this time for a widow. I really love that a widow is involved in this miracle because in that time, widows were low on the social ladder; they were defenseless and had no means of working. God cares for those on the lower rungs of society.

> *"For thus says the Lord God of Israel: 'The bin of flour shall not be used up, nor shall the jar of oil run dry, until the day the Lord sends rain on the earth.'*
> *The bin of flour was not used up, nor did the jar of oil run dry, according to the word of the Lord which He spoke by Elijah."*
> 1 KINGS 17:14,16

The prophet had gone and hidden himself by the brook Cherith at the command of God during a famine that he had prophesied. The time spent at the brook was marked by manifestations of the Spirit. But as the brook dried up, God, by a word of knowledge, told Elijah about a widow in Zaraphath that had been commanded to provide for him. This was quite a test for the widow. Even though God had already spoken to her directly about Elijah's coming visit, she had very little money or possessions. But when she made the choice to obey God, the working of the miraculous fed Elijah *and* her family. God did not just have feeding His prophet in mind.

Elisha, Elijah's spiritual heir, also saw the working of a miracle involving a widow.

This was yet another desperate situation that required divine intervention. We need to have our spiritual eyes open to see that miracles are always in the neighborhood of the impossible.

This widow's husband was one of the sons of the prophets. Her husband had left her in serious debt so that the creditors had threatened to take her two sons as payment. In this state of despair, she came to Elisha.

> *"So Elisha said to her, 'What shall I do for you? Tell me, what do you have in the house?' And she said, 'Your maidservant has nothing in the house but a jar of oil.' Then he said, 'Go, borrow vessels from every-where, from all your neighbors—empty vessels; do not gather just a few.'*
>
> *Now it came to pass, when the vessels were full, that she said to her son, 'Bring me another vessel.' And he said to her, 'There is not another vessel.' So the oil ceased."*
>
> 2 KINGS 4: 2-3,6

The first thing that Elisha did was redirect her focus from her lack to what she had access to. The seed of a miracle is already within the grasp of the one needing a miracle.

In the case of New Testament believers, the Spirit from whom the gift of the working of miracles flows lives on the inside of believers. We need not look to the hills for miracles; we need to look within to the One who is greater!

This widow, like so many believers, did not see the value of what she had and immediately downplayed it—a jar of oil—as "nothing." When we do not see the value of a seed, we miss the possibility of a miracle because all miracles start with a seed. Honor what you have in your hands, no matter how small and insignificant it looks.

Elisha, under the unction of the Spirit, commanded her to go get as many jars as she could find. Her faith and obedience to this would affect the working of the miracle. Our faith and obedience will affect the working of miracles in our lives as well.

The widow gathered all the jars she could get her hands on. The miraculous flow of oil stopped when the availability of the jars ceased. The working of miracles involves a "working,"—a doing, on our part.

The gift of faith receives while the working of miracles works a miracle.

I have organized humanitarian outreaches for many years. In many situations, these events soften the ground in places that would otherwise be closed to the gospel. One time, I had put together a medical mission group to Asia. The team of medical personnel collected and brought medicinal drugs and all kinds of other supplements. We knew from having done these medical outreaches in the past that multivitamins were one of the most popular items to have. The team would bring the pills and medications in large wholesale-style bottles, and then repack them when they landed into smaller sacks for distribution at the clinics. We would give everyone who came a small bag of multivitamins regardless of what they came to the clinics for. Typically, we would put up a tent in a local village and stay there for a week. Sometimes we would see thousands of people per week!

Once, halfway through the week, when we met for prayer in the morning before heading out, I was informed that we had unexpectedly run out of multivitamins. The team was very diligent and kept daily records so they knew exactly what we had, and they knew that the supply would not be enough to even last the day. We still had three days of outreach left, and we hadn't budgeted for the size of the crowds.

There wasn't much more we could do. So, as we got ready to board the bus to the clinic, we left saying among ourselves, "Well, we'll just have to ask God to stretch and multiply what we have."

The crowds that day were as large as the ones we had all week, and when the outreached clinic closed, we were all tired as we made our way back to the hotel. On the bus someone mentioned that somehow we had been able to give everyone who came to the clinic a bag of vitamins. We were all a little surprised but didn't think much of it because we were so tired.

The next morning, when we met for prayer before heading out, we saw that the same bag where the vitamins were usually packed was still full of multivitamins. Inventory of what was used and available was taken daily, so we knew this supply was not accounted for. We were shocked, and I think we were all thinking the same thing, but no one dared say a word.

That evening the team member running the pharmacy once again told us that everyone who had come to the clinic had received multivitamins. And the next morning at team prayer, we once again were surprised to see that the luggage bag that stored the multivitamins was full. This continued for the whole outreach, and by the time the trip was over, we still had so many bags of multivitamins that we had to leave them behind with the pastors.

The Spirit will flow through what we already have to work a miracle.

The working of miracles always flows with what we already have in our possession. There is a "seedtime and harvest" principle to the working of miracles. *The Spirit will flow through what we already have to work a miracle.* That is why there is a "working" of the miracle. What is in hand must be utilized, must be worked.

- The children of Israel had to give up the manna they had collected the previous day and gather fresh manna.

- Moses had to strike the rock.

- It was the clothing that the children of Israel already had on their backs and the sandals already on their feet that were preserved for forty years as they wandered the desert.

- The donkey that Balaam rode on was the one that saw the angel of the Lord and then spoke.

- The widow of Zarapeth had to reach for the last of the flour to make a meal for the prophet and her family.

- Jesus filled the pots with water before turning them to wine.

- Jesus used what little food was available to feed the multitudes.

THE POWER GIFTS RAISE THE DEAD

Undoubtedly, one sure miracle is when the dead are raised. This extraordinary miracle is tied to, yet distinct from, the gifts of healings in that to bring a person back from the dead, one of the gifts of healings is required. Otherwise whatever caused the death will immediately bring death about again. Then it takes the gift of faith to step out and receive the miracle. Finally, the working of miracles calls back the departed's spirit and breathes life back into the body.

"The blind see and the lame walk; the lepers are cleansed and the deaf hear; the dead are raised up and the poor have the gospel preached to them."

MATTHEW 11:5

Raising the dead was one of the specific miracles that Jesus used to identify Himself to John the Baptist. This was clearly part of the command of Jesus to the disciples as they were commissioned to go preach the gospel.

"And as you go, preach, saying, 'The kingdom of heaven is at hand.' Heal the sick, cleanse the lepers, raise the dead, cast out demons. Freely you have received, freely give."

MATTHEW 10:7-8

Yet we see that Jesus did not raise *all* the dead. He did not even raise John the Baptist when news arrived that he had been executed. The early Church, likewise, did not attempt to raise Stephen, the first martyr, or even James when he was executed by Herod. Like all the other gifts of the Spirit, the working of miracles is initiated by the Spirit.

Smith Wigglesworth, the famed British apostle of faith, is reported to have raised quite a few people from the dead—including his wife! John G. Lake, known as an apostle to Africa, also records raising his sister from the dead. In more recent history, evangelist Reinhard Bonnke, who recorded nearly eighty million decisions for Christ in his crusades, also has reports of the dead being raised. And they are not the only ones with such reports in our time.

NATURE BOWS TO THE WORKING OF MIRACLES

Perhaps the biblical miracle most commonly portrayed in cinema is Moses' parting of the Red Sea.

The children of Israel escaping Pharaoh's army through the Red Sea was one of the first miracles that displayed God's power to deliver His people over the laws of nature. There had been miracles over nature displayed in the ten plagues of Egypt, but this miracle was not just a sign like those. It was a direct response from God to save and deliver His people.

Trapped between mountains and the Red Sea, it seemed that the wrath of Pharaoh's army was certain. They knew that there would be no mercy. The instruction of God to Moses was typical of those that accompany the gift of the working of miracles:

> *"But lift up your rod, and stretch out your hand over the sea and divide it. And the children of Israel shall go on dry ground through the midst of the sea."*
>
> EXODUS 14:16

The working of miracles always involves something you have in your hand, and it always involves yielding that to the Lord. You must "work" the miracle!

Had Moses not lifted his rod and stretched his hand over the sea, the Red Sea would not have divided. Then, after the sea was divided, the children of Israel had to physically walk across to complete the miracle of deliverance and protection.

There were so many other ways God could have chosen to do this. He could have just confounded Pharaoh's army. He could have transported the children of Israel through the air like He did with Phillip in the book of Acts. He could have enabled the children of Israel to walk on water. But God chose to have Moses lift his rod, stretch out his hand over the sea, and then have the people walk across the ocean floor. The gift of the working of miracles, given as the Spirit wills, will always come with instructions that must be followed for the miracle to manifest. There is always a practical aspect for the working of miracles to manifest.

Joshua received some detailed, practical instructions from God before the walls of Jericho.

> *"You shall march around the city, all you men of war; you shall go all around the city once. This you shall do six days. And seven priests shall bear seven trumpets of rams' horns before the ark. But the seventh day you shall march around the city seven times, and the priests shall blow the trumpets. It shall come to pass, when they make a long blast with the ram's horn, and when you hear the sound of the trumpet, that all the people shall shout with a great shout; then the wall of the city will fall down flat...."*
>
> JOSHUA 6:3-5

Of course, we know what happened in that story. The walls came down. But the point here is that the miracle would not have happened had the instructions not been followed. Now, granted, the instructions had no actual bearing on the walls falling down. Walls do not normally fall down because of people marching around them for a couple of days. So, it wasn't the marching or shouting that brought the walls down; it was the obedience to the instructions that caused the miracle. Marching around and then shouting on the last day was the "working" side of the miracle.

The working of miracles always starts with "working" instructions before the miracle manifests.

THE WORKING OF CREATIVE MIRACLES

"Now as Jesus passed by, He saw a man who was blind from birth. And His disciples asked Him, saying, 'Rabbi, who sinned, this man or his parents, that he was born blind?' Jesus answered, 'Neither this man nor his parents sinned, but that the works of God should be revealed in him. I must work the works of Him who sent Me while it is day; the night is coming when no one can work. As long as I am in the world, I am the light of the world.' When He had said these things, He spat on the ground and made clay with the saliva; and He anointed the eyes of the blind man with the clay. And He said to him, 'Go, wash in the pool of Siloam' (which is translated, Sent). So he went and washed, and came back seeing."

JOHN 9:1-7

The working of miracles, like all the other gifts of the Spirit, requires the leading of the Spirit to be entered into. We have no other references of such instructions for a miracle, nor do we have instructions to replicate these steps. Can you imagine the altar call at church if we did? "Come on up here

145

if you are sick, and we'll spit on you to make mud to rub in your eyes!" Now, I am not saying God could not lead you to do that, but if He did, that would be the exception, not the rule.

The making of mud is reminiscent of how God created the bodies of Adam and Eve in Eden.

The natural, when submitted to the Spirit, becomes a conduit for the supernatural.

Again, this speaks to how the natural, when submitted to the Spirit, becomes a conduit for the supernatural. The (formerly) blind man himself had instructions that had to be followed; he had to go wash in the pool of Siloam. We can only imagine what would have happened if he had decided to rinse off somewhere else—even from a vessel of drinking water instead. Could Jesus not have spoken over him or just laid hands on him as He had done with others? The Spirit is so intricately involved in our lives that specific instructions are given for specific individuals. This is how personal the Holy Spirit is with us. He has specifics for us.

"And a certain man lame from his mother's womb was carried, whom they laid daily at the gate of the temple which is called Beautiful, to ask alms from those who entered the temple; who, seeing Peter and John about to go into the temple, asked for alms. And fixing his

eyes on him, with John, Peter said, 'Look at us.' So he gave them his attention, expecting to receive something from them. Then Peter said, 'Silver and gold I do not have, but what I do have I give you: In the name of Jesus Christ of Nazareth, rise up and walk.' And he took him by the right hand and lifted him up, and immediately his feet and ankle bones received strength."

ACTS 3:2-7

This man, being lame from birth, was not even expecting a miracle. He was simply begging scraps to live. You could say that he had settled into the lifestyle of being a professional beggar. He was by the temple not seeking supernatural help from God but seeking scraps to get through the day. This miracle was not initiated by his faith or asking but by the grace and mercy of God. Like all good things, God is the initiator. *Our faith can only take what His grace first offers.*

The gift of the working of miracles was stirred so greatly in Peter when he was approached for alms that he was drawn to the beggar and commanded him saying, "Look at us." Like Elisha had done with the widow in Second Kings, Peter had to take the man's attention off his current plight in order to offer him something better. What we focus on is important because that is what becomes magnified.

As long as the widow focused on her "nothing" or this man focused on being "lame," it would have hindered their ability to receive. What they focused on would not have changed God's willingness or ability to bring transformation, but they would not have been in position to receive what was offered.

Shift your sights to the supernatural. Choose to see what God can do rather than what is in front of you. Faith sees what grace offers!

Shift your sights to the supernatural. Choose to see what God can do rather than what is in front of you. Faith sees what grace offers!

The "working" part to this manifestation of the working of miracles was the command from Peter for the lame man to "rise and walk" then grabbing and lifting him up. *The gift of the working of miracles is always bold in expression!*

One night, toward the end of a service, as I was getting close to handing the service back to the pastors, I kept having the word *pins* come up as I prayed in tongues. I kept checking my spirit to see if I was to do anything along the lines of calling people up for prayer, but nothing came except the word *pins*. It came so strongly in my spirit that I started saying it out loud. I must have said it forcefully ten times or more.

The congregation quieted down and watched me expectantly, but I had no leading to do anything with the word. So I just kept saying, "Pins. Something about pins."

Someone in the front section shouted, "Do you mean like acupuncture?"

The pastor's wife answered back, "No, that's not what he means."

I laughed and said, "The only thing I am getting is to say *pins*. That's all I've got."

So the worship team started singing, and I handed the service back to the pastors. The next morning, I got a long email from my office that was also copied to the church office. This man said he had felt he needed to be in the service the night before, but he had been held up at work and decided to watch the live stream from home instead. He got back a little later than expected, and after catching the service halfway through, he saw the part where I was saying *pins*. He didn't think much of it (neither did most people at the service), but that night when he was in bed, he felt warmth on his ankle. I had been to this church many times, and so they all remembered me saying that I sometimes would sense the anointing on parts of my body as a warmth. Many people in those services had also sensed the same warmth. I would not teach this as doctrine, but I am reporting it as my experience.

This man sensed a heat on his ankle, but after drifting off to sleep,he was awoken by what felt like his leg muscles and sinews moving around. He ignored it and went back to sleep, but when he awoke, he thought about his unusual night. He felt around his calf and ankle and excitedly had his wife, a massage therapist, do the same. In high school, he had broken bones in his leg and had to have orthopedic pins inserted; he also had to have a metal plate put in, but it had been so long ago that he could no longer feel them.

The pins and the plate had dissolved overnight! He contacted us later and told us that his doctor verified the fact.

The pins and the plate had dissolved overnight! He contacted us later and told us that his doctor verified the fact.

The working of miracles can dissolve metal pins.

The working of miracles can operate by the simple act of saying, *pins.*

The working of miracles can operate long distance—there is no distance in the spirit.

One of my favorite times to minister is when we host conferences because a lot of pastors and ministers come from all around to attend them. When people come to a meeting with that type of expectation and determination, you know they are going to get what they came for.

Before the last service of one of these conferences, I was standing down front visiting with some people before they made their way back to their seats. During this time, I saw a lady standing timidly to the side. I motioned for her to come over, and she told me that she was a pastor's wife. She had come by bus from over six hours away because she had heard about these conferences from a friend. She came to the first service early to get a seat up front.

Now, I walk around a lot when I minister, and that evening during the service, I walked over to the section where this woman was sitting. I had never met her before, and I don't even remember doing this. But she described later that as I was preaching and passing by where she sat, I laid my hands on her shoulder and continued teaching. Then just as I was going to move on, I looked at her and said, "Bless you! All whole in Jesus' name."

Before she had come to the conference, her doctor had advised against it because of the severity of the cancer in her body. There was an open, bleeding sore on her breast. She said that it bled so much that every time she had to change her undergarments, they would be stained with blood. She also had water in her lungs, and the doctor had said that she might not even make the six-hour bus journey.

This was a desperate situation, but at the very first service, as she sat in the front section, I had walked over to her. That very afternoon when she went back to her room to rest before services, the bleeding sore had closed up! By that evening, she was breathing clearly, and after she went back to her doctors she learned that the cancer had disappeared as well.

Thank God for the spiritual gift of the working of miracles!

Chapter Six

PROPHECY

"To another prophecy...."
1 Corinthians 12:10

Of the three gifts of inspiration, the simple gift of prophecy is the one to be most desired. This is because this single gift is equal to the gifts of diverse kinds of tongues and the interpretation of tongues combined. Think of how it takes two five dollar bills to equal ten dollars. Or you could just have a single ten dollar bill. Paul put it this way, "For he who prophesies is greater than he who speaks with tongues, unless indeed he interprets, that the church may receive edification" (1 Cor. 14:5). So, we see the way Paul put a value on the gifts was based on the edification received by the Church.

As we have already seen by looking at the gift of the word of wisdom and the word of knowledge, the element of revelation and predictive foretelling is contained in those two manifestations. Those were the gifts of the Spirit that all the Old Testament prophets operated in.

In the New Testament, even those who have the gift of the word of knowledge, the gift of the word of wisdom, or the gift of prophecy do not always stand in the office of a prophet (Eph. 4:11). These nine gifts in First Corinthians 12 are available to all believers. Those five offices in Ephesians 4 are specific categories. Apostles, prophets, evangelists, pastors, and teachers move in the same gifts as all believers but at a different intensity of anointing and regularity. Prophesying once or twice doesn't qualify someone for the office of a prophet.

The New Testament gift of prophecy is not predictive, rather, it's meant to uplift.

> *"But he who prophesies speaks edification and exhortation and comfort to men."*
>
> 1 CORINTHIANS 14:3

The New Testament gift of prophecy is not predictive, rather, it's meant to uplift.

Guidance and direction are not among the listed functions of prophecy.

One way the Old Testament was different from the New Testament is in the role of the Holy Spirit. In the Old Testament, the Holy Spirit rested upon three main categories of people: priests, prophets, and kings. And even then, it was temporary since no one in the Old Testament was born again as a new creation. The Holy Spirit was *on* them, but He did not dwell *in* them. In the Old Testament, the prophets primarily provided direction through the Word of the Lord to the people of God.

In the New Testament, because believers already had the Holy Spirit living on the inside of them, they did not go to prophets for direction; those moving in prophetic gifts provided clarification and amplification only.

Edification, exhortation, and comfort also do not include criticism, rebuke, or the public exposing of wrongs. New Testament prophecy *always* encourages, always uplifts. I have seen people try to dress up their opinion of what someone else should do in the guise of a prophetic utterance. Or, just as bad, use a "thus saith the Lord" to say what they think of someone. Correction in the New Testament comes from the preaching and teaching of God's Word.

Inspired utterances can include prophecy, but not all inspired utterance *is* prophecy. Many times, when a minister is preaching or teaching under the anointing, there is an element of prophecy to it.

It is easy to tell when a minister flows off notes they prepared for a message and when they step into inspired utterance. There is a tangible shift that comes into the room when that happens. Obviously, I tell ministers that it is important to study and prepare themselves before they preach and teach— and there is nothing wrong with ministering from notes either—but we should not be so dependent upon our notes that we ignore the Holy Spirit's nudging while we minister. I have been guilty of this, where I was so stuck on my well-prepared notes that I didn't make room for anything the Holy Spirit wanted to say.

I've had some pastors ask, "Why couldn't the Holy Spirit just tell me everything to minister on while I am preparing my messages?" Simply put, an element of the gift of prophecy is inspired speech. This means that you will receive inspiration for that moment, in that moment. And this doesn't just apply to those preaching. I've told businesspeople the same thing. You can prepare for that sales presentation all night but make room for the Holy Spirit to jump in while you are presenting.

Prophecy, or any of the gifts of the Spirit, do not contain or convey revelation on par with the written, recorded verses of God's Word. This is the New Testament pattern. On the day of Pentecost, when the Holy Spirit was poured out in glorious power, what happened right after was that Peter stood to speak under the anointing of the Spirit and immediately verified the occurrence with the writings of the prophet Joel. So the outpouring of the Spirit on the day of Pentecost did not add to Scripture, but rather, it was confirmed and contained by what Scripture already said.

Even though prophecy edifies, exhorts, and comforts, this is not to mean that all you need do is walk around with a positive attitude, a big smile, and be nice to everyone with an encouraging word. I am not saying that's not a good thing to do, but it's just not the gift of prophecy. Like all the other spiritual gifts, true prophecy must have an element of divine inspiration, not just natural inclination. Just like you wouldn't say all medical doctors have the gifts of healings, you cannot say that someone who is friendly and kind is operating in the gift of prophecy. They might be, but being friendly in itself is not an aspect of the gift of prophecy.

Inspired utterance is a feature of any of the gifts of the Spirit that are expressed verbally.

The gift of prophecy balances the weighing scales to the ministry of the teacher. Edification, exhortation, and comfort primarily minister to the arena of a person's emotions just as a teacher ministers to a person's intellect. Both the emotions and intellect are functions of the human soul.

Prophecy has a way of enlivening the enlightenment that teachers bring.

Prophecy has a way of enlivening the enlightenment that teachers bring.

We see these two functions of prophecy and teaching operating in Antioch (Acts 13:1), and they produced a beautifully balanced ministry together. Just as teaching stems superstitious fanaticism, prophecy challenges dead, dry intellectualism.

In First Corinthians 14:31, we see the gift of prophecy tied into our learning. "For you can all prophesy one by one, that all may learn and all may be encouraged."

So, those set in the office of teacher will uplift with what they teach. Since God speaks through the gifts of prophecy, and since prophecy is edification, exhortation, and comfort, when the gift of prophecy teaches, you could also say that all inspired teaching will edify, exhort, and comfort. Be wary of any teaching that does not uplift you. The washing of the water of God's Word will always leave you refreshed, even as it corrects and disciplines you.

The human will and faith are involved in delivering and receiving prophecy but not human reasoning.

Prophecy is mentioned over twenty times in the Corinthian letters alone. It was widely taught by Paul because of its great need in the Body of Christ. Church history points to this as well. When there was a lack of prophecy, the Dark Ages ensued. When there was a lack of teaching, Gnosticism and sensationalism reared their heads.

A genuine move of God always involves faith enough for the operations of the Spirit to flow, but it is always hand in hand with determined obedience to the will of God as revealed in the Scriptures. The balance of the Word and the Spirit is the hallmark of any move of the Spirit.

Through the gift of prophecy, our Father puts His arms around us in a heavenly embrace.

The gift of prophecy reveals the heart of the Father toward His children. Our Father's heart is always to edify, exhort, and comfort us. That is why it takes a walk with God to flow in the gift of prophecy at its highest level. Through the gift of prophecy, our Father puts His arms around us in a heavenly embrace. Jeremiah said it best: "But His word was in my heart like a burning fire shut up in my bones; I was weary holding it back" (Jer. 20:9). This is the burning heart that accompanies prophecy.

Propheteia (Strong's 4394), the Greek word used here "signifies the speaking forth of the mind and counsel of God" (Vine's Expository Dictionary of New Testament Words). So, we see that there is a flowing downward from God to the person exercising the gift, then to the one receiving the utterance. Much of the book of Psalms fits into this category. Prophecy has a sense of speaking for another. It is an intermediary, a spokesperson's position.

PROPHETS AND PROPHESYING

In Acts 21, we see an interesting contrast between two levels of prophetic functioning.

Paul, entering Caesarea, stayed with Phillip the evangelist. We are then told that, "This man had four virgin daughters *who prophesied*"(Acts 21:9). These four daughters were not prophets, but they were simply known to prophesy. They moved in the gift of prophecy; they spoke words of edification, exhortation, and comfort.

But then, right in the very next verse, we see the function of a New Testament prophet.

"And as we stayed many days, a certain prophet named Agabus came down from Judea. When he had come to us, he took Paul's belt, bound his own hands and feet,

and said, 'Thus says the Holy Spirit, "So shall the Jews at Jerusalem bind the man who owns this belt, and deliver him into the hands of the Gentiles."'''

ACTS 21:10-11

Unlike Philip's four daughters, Agabus did not just prophesy; he was actually called a prophet.

The prophetic word he delivered to Paul carried the weight of a word of wisdom, since he spoke of things to come. The word of wisdom, in this case, could have flowed through the gift of prophecy as he spoke to Paul, or Agabus may have received the word of wisdom earlier and just then reported it to Paul at Phillip's house. However, he provided no direction to Paul. By the Spirit, he simply told Paul what awaited him in Jerusalem. Paul had to decide what to do. Paul was not led by personal prophecy. New Testament prophets informed and confirmed, but they did not direct. That is the job of the Holy Spirit living inside of us.

New Testament prophets informed and confirmed, but they did not direct. That is the job of the Holy Spirit living inside of us.

Paul said that we know in part, and we prophesy in part (1 Cor. 13:9). So, we see here that the Holy Spirit bore witness with Paul that imprisonment and trials awaited him in Jerusalem (Acts 20:22, 23). Paul said that he did not know all the things that were going to happen to him there (Acts 21:22); he may have generally known what was going to happen, but he did not know the details. No prophecy, no matter how accurate and detailed, comes as a complete picture. Remember, it is always a word of wisdom, a word of knowledge, and, you could say, a word of prophecy.

Now, even though Paul had a witness from the Spirit of what was going to happen in Jerusalem, Agabus gave more details about what would happen when he prophesied to Paul. Agabus added the detail that Paul would be delivered to the Gentiles (Acts 20:11). Paul was edified by this prophecy. It was a confirmation of what he had already received, and it prepared him for what was to come.

SONGS, PRAYERS, AND WORSHIP

"My soul magnifies the Lord,
And my spirit has rejoiced in God my Savior.
For He has regarded the lowly state of His
maidservant;
For behold, henceforth all generations will call me
blessed.
For He who is mighty has done great things for me,
And holy is His name.
And His mercy is on those who fear Him
From generation to generation.
He has shown strength with His arm;
He has scattered the proud in the imagination of their
hearts.

He has put down the mighty from their thrones,
And exalted the lowly.
He has filled the hungry with good things,
And the rich He has sent away empty.
He has helped His servant Israel,
In remembrance of His mercy,
As He spoke to our fathers,
To Abraham and to his seed forever."

LUKE 1:46-55

We see this simple gift of prophecy eloquently expressed through Mary, the mother of Jesus, when she exclaimed the Magnificat, commonly called the Song of Mary. Only once (in verse 48) is there a stepping over into the predictive word of wisdom. The rest of this inspired song was just an uplifting, exuberant praise to God.

In Psalm 5, David utters an entire prayer that is a Holy Ghost-inspired prophecy. It uplifts and stirs me every time I read it. You'll be blessed reading the whole book of Psalms, but consider these closing verses:

"But let all those rejoice who put their trust in You;
Let them ever shout for joy, because You defend them;
Let those also who love Your name be joyful in You.
For You, O Lord, will bless the righteous; with favor
You will surround him as with a shield."

PSALM 5:11-12

Later on, in Psalm 8, the gift of prophecy through David flows as worship. This deeply reverential psalm worshipfully describes the majesty of God and stirs faith in the reader, showing us how big God really is. In other words, it exhorts, edifies, and comforts the listeners.

The opening two verses start out:

> *"O Lord, our Lord, how excellent is Your name in all the earth, who have set Your glory above the heavens. Out of the mouth of babes and nursing infants You have ordained strength, because of Your enemies, That You may silence the enemy and the avenger."*
>
> PSALM 8:1-2

Even a quick read through these inspired songs and prayers show how much beauty and depth flows from the simple gift of prophecy. I am sure you have experienced this just as I have.

We have all experienced a moment when someone is praying—or even worshipping—and then one song or stanza will seem to swoop into the room and come alive. The gift of prophecy can flow through inspired utterances of any kind.

PROPHECY: SUPERNATURALLY SPEAKING

We make a mistake if we think that God only speaks to forewarn with predictions or to demand a holy life. As our Father, God primarily speaks with us to communicate, fellowship, and bring instruction for our growth and correction. When we see God accurately as Father, we begin to understand the absurdity of thinking that He only warns or rebukes. What would we think of an earthly father if that's the sum of his communication with his children? Our heavenly Father wants to communicate His love to His children, and the gift of prophecy is that channel. The gift of prophecy is an expression of our Father's desire to edify, exhort, and comfort us.

> When we see God accurately as Father, we begin to understand the absurdity of thinking that He only warns or rebukes.

To *edify* literally means "to build up." Jesus used this same term when He said He was going to build His Church. *So through the gift of prophecy, Jesus builds the Church by building us.* Since prophecy edifies us, builds us up, and Jesus said He was building up the Church, that would mean that to lay aside the gift of prophecy would be to lay aside one of the means by which Jesus builds the Church. This is why we are pointedly told, "Do not despise prophecies" (1 Thess. 5:20).

The word *exhortation* means "a calling near." In the original Greek, it has the same root meaning from which we get the word *comforter.* This is one of the descriptive titles mentioned by Jesus for the Holy Spirit. You cannot call someone near with rebuke or harsh tones. The Holy Spirit is portrayed as a dove, not a vulture. He is gentle. And the Holy Spirit calls us to draw near to the Father's presence.

I was once told of a visiting minister who called himself a prophet, but all he did was rant and rave about the "sin in the land" and berate the people in attendance for a lack of fervency for God. The irony is that those in attendance did have a fervency for God; otherwise, why would they be at the meeting? It seemed like he was preaching to the wrong crowd. The Holy Spirit does not kick us into the Father's presence. He woos us gently and lovingly.

The Holy Spirit does not kick us into the Father's presence. He woos us gently and lovingly.

Sometimes in obeying the will of God, believers can be tempted to feel that they are walking alone. This leads to self-pity and isolation. It can even cause believers to back off completely from the will of God. This is when a word of prophecy can come into their lives to exhort them and encourage them with the truth of God walking alongside them. With the flow of exhortation through the gift of prophecy, it ushers a stronger awareness of the presence of God into the lives of believers receiving prophecy. It imparts a blessing and a boost of strength to stay the course and finish the race.

"Consolation, solace and comfort in trial or distress" is the meaning of *comfort*, and it is the third definition of the function of the gift of prophecy. There are always depressed and saddened people around us. The answer isn't always in medication or casting out demons, although both have their place. God can uplift the downtrodden with a supernatural word of comfort through the gift of prophecy.

When believers following the will of God for their lives turn aside or stumble along the way, it is the gift of prophecy manifesting in its third operation that brings comfort to them. The purpose of comfort is to soothe the pain of missing the mark—or even the muscle aches of staying the course—encouraging the believer to continue on with God.

This aspect of exhortation and comfort has even help me on my international flights.

I travel a lot between Southeast Asia and America. Back then, the transit point on those long fights was Japan. I would normally have a few hours between flights in that airport, and I enjoyed my time there. But if my flight from that airport got delayed, it would affect all my other connections. It was usually fine, but one time going to Southeast Asia from America, I had to catch a tight connection and be ready to speak almost right after I landed. I don't usually prefer those types of tight connections, but the schedule just couldn't be moved.

As I waited for my flight in the airport lounge, an announcement came on that my flight was cancelled because of weather. All passengers were instructed to make their way to the airline agents to see if alternative flights could be booked. By the time I got to the counter, there was a long line of angry people speaking loudly to the lady behind the counter. As much as I travel, I have never understood why passengers get upset with counter staff over delays or cancellations. I always think if there is a problem with the plane or the flight path, I see it as a blessing for them to *not* put us on the plane.

Still, the people in front of me were quite upset, and the lady seemed a little shaken. I felt sorry for her, and by the time it was my turn at the counter, I just quietly handed her my travel documents and waited. She meekly told me that there was not a flight available yet, but that she would let me know as soon as there was.

I stood to the side and decided I would stay there for a bit longer before heading back to the airport lounge. I got on my phone and tried calling the hosting pastors to let them know I would likely miss the services.

After the lines and tempers had died down, I sensed the nudge of the Holy Spirit to go talk to the airline lady at the counter. I hesitated because I was physically tired and still had a few more calls to make, but the push of the Spirit just kept getting stronger until I heard the Lord tell me, "Go up to her. Tell her she is doing a good job and that everything is okay."

I slowly made my way to the counter and had her look at my travel documents again. She repeated what she had said earlier, instructing me to wait. As I took my travel documents back from her, I simply said, "You know, considering all that is happening, you are doing a great job. Everything is okay."

She looked up at me with a surprised look and then quietly thanked me. I went back to my seat and started making calls again. In a few minutes, out of the corner of my eye, I saw her making her way toward me.

"Dr. Tan?" she said, "Can I see your boarding pass again, please?"

I gave it her, and she typed the information into her tablet. After a moment, she leaned over to me and asked if I would follow her. We went around back, and she told me that there was another flight leaving in one hour, and although it only had one seat left, she had gotten me on that flight. Then she added, "Thank you for the encouragement. I needed it."

Those other angrier passengers were going to the same destination I was, but favor and the word of prophecy moved that one seat in my direction.

I cannot overstate this: all aspects of the gift of prophecy point and pull us upward. Anything that does not, is not prophecy.

> *"But if all prophesy, and an unbeliever or an uninformed person comes in, he is convinced by all, he is convicted by all. And thus, the secrets of his heart are revealed; and so, falling down on his face, he will worship God and report that God is truly among you."*
> 1 CORINTHIANS 14:24-25

All aspects of the gift of prophecy point and pull us upward. Anything that does not, is not prophecy.

Paul goes on to instruct us concerning the gift of prophecy: although it is primarily geared toward believers, it also has an effect on the unbeliever. This must be because the understanding is able to connect with what is spoken through prophecy and, as we've said, prophecy connects with the emotions.

THE FLOW OF PROPHECY

The gift of prophecy is the merging of man's intellect and the mind of the Spirit. Prophecy is where the mind of man meets the mind of God. Then, at that meeting, the mind of man yields to the mind of God and allows for the mind of God to express His thoughts through man's vocal capacities. So, in a very real way, prophecy is the perfect God speaking through an imperfect vessel.

If it were not for man's involvement, all prophecy would be perfect. God's only limitation in communication with mankind is mankind itself. We require language and no language is perfect.

I am monolingual. English is the only language I am fluent in. So, I am very familiar with working with interpreters when I minister in foreign lands. And I can testify that having a reliable interpreter can make all the difference ministering in a foreign service. In a way, when I am preaching in places where an interpreter is required, the congregation is actually listening to the interpreter and not me.

I was in a service one time where I had excitedly declared, "Jesus is Lord! Jesus is Lord! Jesus is Lord!"

The interpreter next to me timidly whispered, "Jesus is Lord…."

I nudged him to repeat exactly what I had said, and he looked up and replied, "Yes… yes… it is the same."

No, it definitely was not the same. That was a particularly short service. It did not matter how enthusiastically I was preaching; my words had to flow through my interpreter.

The three gifts of inspiration—prophecy, different kinds of tongues, and interpretation of tongues—and the three gifts of revelation—the word of wisdom, the word of knowledge, and discerning of spirits—are all products of the coming together of God and the believer. The infallibility of God and the fallibility of the believer intermingle for these gifts to manifest. Even with Spirit-filled believers, their personalities will still peek through in how they express these manifestations.

Yielding to the Holy Spirit can be learned in prayer, renewing the mind, and obedience to the promptings of the Spirit received throughout the day. Knowing the Holy Spirit is the key to yielding to Him. This is something we can and must be developed in.

Knowing the Holy Spirit is the key to yielding to Him. This is something we can and must be developed in.

PROPHECY HOUSE RULES

Of all the gifts listed in First Corinthians 12, some of the most detailed instructions for their use in the Church are for the vocal gifts of inspiration. This is probably because these manifestations are incorporated into the structure of the service itself, and since they are vocal gifts meant to be spoken aloud, they immediately draw attention to themselves. Also, because prophecy can stir the emotions of its hearers, prophecy has the potential to be manipulative.

I have seen this type of abuse happen before. There are ministries that guarantee you a prophecy if you will call in with your credit card ready. Now, I believe in prophecies, *and* I believe in sowing into ministries as the Lord leads. I also believe that you should partner with ministries that feed you spiritually. But what you should *not* do is call a 1-800 number with your credit card ready just because you were promised a prophetic reimbursement.

Below is another instruction Paul gave us with further instruction on prophetic exercise within the Church.

> *"Let two or three prophets speak, and let the others judge."*
>
> 1 CORINTHIANS 14:29

In most churches today, this instruction would not be necessary because they rarely have even one prophet speaking. But the church in Corinth had so many prophets wanting to speak that Paul had to limit the number allowed. Clearly, it is the New Testament pattern that prophets speaking should be part of a regular church gathering. This doesn't mean that there *must* be a prophetic utterance every time the church gathers, but it does mean that we should be prepared for it and make room for when the anointing flows that way.

Practically, having more than two or three prophets speak would dilute the impact of the messages they uttered. Since each prophecy is, in essence, the Lord speaking, then it would also make sense that we would need to process and assimilate any words that came forth.

When should the prophets have spoken? Should they just have yelled out whatever the Lord told them whenever He moved on them? I love the practical way that Paul regulated the manifestations of the Spirit in a service. Since God is a God of order and not confusion, it would be against the His nature to have prophetic utterances come forth at points in the service where it would intrude on the rest of the service. Paul put it this way: "And the spirits of the prophets are subject to the prophets" (1 Cor. 14:32). This means that the one receiving the prophecy had control over when that prophecy is released.

God sets leadership in place and that includes in a service. If someone receives a word that he or she feel needs to be shared with the congregation, the individual should make his or her way to the leadership and submit that word to them to see if they feel that word should be released at that time. If not, then the responsibility is lifted off the congregant, and from that point on, it's between God and the leadership.

I will add that from what I've observed at the many prayer meetings I've led where people wait on the presence of the Lord is that God speaks to many people in that environment, but not everything He says needs to be shared publicly. I've ministered at meetings where after about forty-five minutes of being in the presence of God, someone came up to the front, took the microphone and said, "The Lord is saying, 'I am here.'"

That was not necessary to say. We all knew God was there because we all sensed Him. That might have been a word to that individual or it might just have been him or her sensing God's presence in the room. But it was not necessary to share it publicly because it did not add to the meeting or profit anyone. Remember, the gifts are supposed to profit all. "But the manifestation of the Spirit is given to each one for the profit of all" (1 Cor. 12:7).

I have seen worship leaders do the same thing. They lead the people into the presence of God, then as the people were basking there, the worship leader announces, "The Lord says, 'Worship Me.'"

I almost wanted to ask out loud, "What have we been doing all this time?"

Prophecy is not stating the obvious!

 Prophecy is not stating the obvious!

Here is how we know this gift of prophecy can be increased. Romans 12:6 says, "Having then gifts differing according to the grace that is given to us, let us use them: if prophecy, *let us prophesy in proportion to our faith.*"

If we prophesy in proportion to our faith, and our faith grows, so would our ability to prophesy. God tells us clearly that faith comes by hearing (Rom. 10:17). So, when we hear God's Word, faith comes. As faith comes, the propensity to prophesy increases. Prophecy starts with the written Word and becomes the spoken word.

The flow of edification, exhortation, and comfort can flow so seamlessly that we enter a state of continual availability to dispense inspired utterances. We can be speaking words of life everywhere we go.

> *"Pursue love, and desire spiritual gifts, but especially that you may prophesy."*
> 1 CORINTHIANS 14:1

Chapter Seven

DISCERNING OF SPIRITS

"…To another discerning of spirits…."

1 CORINTHIANS 12:10

The discerning of spirits is one of the three gifts of revelation; this tells us that it reveals *something*, but it has a very limited range compared to the other two gifts of revelation. It differs from the word of wisdom and the word of knowledge in that the object of its revelation, as well as its operation, is entirely spiritual. The word of wisdom and the word of knowledge reveal natural things, past, present, or future. But with the discerning of spirits, the scope of revelation is restricted to a single category.

The word *diakrisis* (Strong's 1253) means "judging through." It also means, "Judging by evidence whether they are evil or of God" (Vine's Expository Dictionary of New Testament Words). So essentially, the basic purpose of this word is to form a judgment based on a piercing of all that is simply outward into the inner, true nature, and seeing right through. This is a sharp word describing a powerful gift.

This ability of "judging through" is one of God's own attributes. By this aspect of His character, the Father executes perfect judgment in all things over all beings. God is omniscient. He knows all things. He doesn't just see all things; He knows the true nature of what is seen. This is what qualifies God to be the ultimate judge of the world.

In light of God's ability to judge by discerning rightly, the book of Hebrews gives us an important avenue through which we can judge:

> *"For the word of God is living and powerful, and sharper than any two-edged sword, piercing even to the division of soul and spirit, and of joints and marrow, and is a discerner of the thoughts and intents of the heart."*
>
> HEBREWS 4:12

The Word of God is imbued with the ability to dissect and discern. When we get the Word of God into us through study and meditation, our minds become renewed so that we can clearly know God's thoughts in a situation and even have His thoughts as our own! *We can think the way God thinks.* Through tongues and interpretation, the Lord said to me, *"If you think like I think, you will manifest like I manifest."*

No believer is left exposed to deception without the defense of the gift of discerning spirits.

With this ability to judge rightly, no believer is left exposed to deception without the defense of the gift of discerning spirits. God has not left us open to deception. God has put in place a spiritual mechanism to show us the truth from the lie. As believers, our first line of defense is always what the Word of God says. You can always receive from the Word of God immediately what the manifestations of the Spirit can bring by the will of the Spirit!

> *"Then Jesus, being filled with the Holy Spirit, returned from the Jordan and was led by the Spirit into the wilderness, being tempted for forty days by the devil...."*
>
> LUKE 4:1-2

Jesus discerned accurately that this experience was satanic in nature. It's important to know who your enemy is in a fight. This enemy could even quote scripture, but Jesus knew who he was and enough of the Scriptures to know that the verses the enemy used were quoted out of context. The discerning of spirits exposed Satan, and when Jesus declared, "It is written," He disarmed his foe! The Word and the Spirit work hand in hand.

What the discerning of spirits gives us is sight into the secret realm of spirits. It can reveal the kind of spirit that is working through a person while he or she manifests supernatural knowledge or power. It supernaturally transmits information that could not be known outside of the manifestation. Through this single operation, we can know the true source and nature of all supernatural manifestations, whether from the throne room or the satanic realm. The source of such spiritual manifestation can only be determined by the use of this gift.

Like all the other gifts, there is nothing natural about it. There is no snooping, prying, "asking around," calculated guessing, cold reading, or investigations involved. *The gift of discerning spirits is not the gift of suspicions.* The discerning of spirits is also not a God-given reason to dislike someone and walk around saying things like, "I discern something wrong with him."

This manifestation is not a reason to spiritualize petty fault finding; *It is primarily sight into the spirit realm.*

Also, this is not just "discernment," as some have said, but the discerning of spirits. There is no spiritual gift called the "gift of discernment." Discernment of people, things, and situations outside of the spirit realm is actually within the jurisdiction of the other two gifts of revelation.

So, since the gift of discerning of spirits lifts the veil into the spiritual realm, it should not *just* reveal demons and evil spirits. The spirit realm is the abode of God, the Holy Spirit, angels, Satan, evil spirits, and the spirit of man. The gift of discerning spirits is not *just* the ability to see evil spirits. Anyone who claims this gift and only sees or senses demons around every corner is only operating under a spirit of "wild imaginations."

However, we should remember that the very existence of this manifestation proves the everyday reality of evil spirits. If all spirits were only good or bad, then why would we have need to discern the spirits? This manifestation is a divine confirmation that there are opposing spiritual forces at work in our earthly realm.

The gift of discerning spirits is not just the ability to see evil spirits.

There is a divine unity to the gifts in manifestation, as we have seen, and that is very much the case with the discerning of spirit. This gift, when in manifestation, has no ability in itself to cast the demonic spirits out or command that they cease their activity. That would require believers exercising the authority given them or the power gifts of either faith, gifts of healings, or the working of miracles.

Also, the discerning of spirits cannot be thought of as a form of spiritual mind reading. This manifestation does not reveal men's thoughts or hearts in the usual sense. If we say someone has a "rebellious spirit," usually what that means is that the person is headstrong and will not submit to leadership. It is the word of knowledge that would reveal that aspect of a man if it was a spiritually motivated problem and not just an untamed soul. This is not the gift of discerning character, thoughts, or hearts. No daytime talk-show-style psychoanalysis is involved. The Holy Spirit is not needed to empower people to be fault-finding or critical.

WHAT THE DISCERNING OF SPIRITS ACCOMPLISHES

As with everything that God does, the gifts of the Spirit are all given a purpose and meant to serve the Church of Jesus Christ in some fashion.

We have already seen that the gift of discerning of spirits allows us to see into the spirit realm. The reason God would want this for us is so that in seeing into that realm, we can distinguish between good and evil by identifying the source of manifestations and motivations.

Distinguishing good from evil is not just needed to protect us outside the Church, but sadly, it can aid us inside the Church as well.

The standard of the Word keeps Church doctrine pure, and the discerning of spirits keeps motives pure!

The standard of the Word keeps Church doctrine pure, and the discerning of spirits keeps motives pure!

It seems like from the very start, the enemy turned up the heat of persecution against the Church to stem its growth, but simultaneously sought to infiltrate and weaken its core message and influence leadership. Part of our defense is in the gift of the discerning of spirits.

Jesus Himself operated in this gift to discern the spirits motivating the people around Him. Jesus was so sharp with this manifestation that in the space of a few verses in Matthew 16, He operated in the discerning of spirits twice with the same person: Peter.

When Peter first identified Jesus as the Christ, "Jesus answered and said to him, 'Blessed are you, Simon Bar-Jonah, for flesh and blood has not revealed this to you, *but My Father who is in heaven*'" (Matt. 16:17).

This was a moment that spiritually shifted mankind. Jesus immediately discerned that it was the Father that brought this revelation. Obviously, Peter did not know he was the recipient of a revelation of such magnitude, but this gift revealed it as the Father Himself.

Interestingly, a very few verses later, Peter again was the oracle from which another utterance came that Jesus quickly judged. This time, after asking who men said He was, Jesus started talking about His coming trial, death, and resurrection. Peter, being quick to speak, advised Jesus against such an idea.

> *"But He turned and said to Peter, 'Get behind Me, Satan! You are an offense to Me, for you are not mindful of the things of God, but the things of men.'"*
> MATTHEW 16:23

Jesus immediately identified Satan speaking. Peter had lots of zeal, a level of spiritual sensitivity, and was always the quickest to share his mind.

Jesus did not put His guard down just because Peter had received a heavenly revelation earlier. He immediately judged by the discerning of spirits. Had Jesus listened to Peter the second time, He would not have gone to the cross for us.

This gift of the Spirit that saved Peter was the same one that he learned to operate in when he matured into a place of early Church leadership. Such Holy Spirit power flowed through Peter and John that Simon, a former sorcerer who came into salvation through the ministry of Phillip, actually offered Peter money to impart his gift to him. Simon's mind was unrenewed, but what did he see that would even cause him to think of such a ridiculous measure? It must have been a great demonstration of power for Simon to pull out his wallet.

Peter was not offended or tempted by this offer of money, nor was he concerned about what others would think. By the discerning of spirits, Peter saw Simon's heart and declared, "You have neither part nor portion in this matter, for *your heart is not right* in the sight of God" (Acts 8:21).

Many believers are unsure about the idea of judging. "Are we ever supposed to judge?" they ask.

To that, I give a resounding, "Yes!"

We are supposed to always *judge situations* but we are *to never judge people*. We never judge the person because we never really know where they are coming from or what pressures persuaded them to act the way they did. We also cannot see their hearts, and therefore, we cannot see their true essence. However, we must always judge situations based on their fruit. It's a simple rule: Believers judge situations but never people.

It's a simple rule: Believers judge situations but never people.

With this gift in operation, Peter did not have to judge the situation because he saw Simon's heart.

Jesus called John the Baptist the greatest of the Old Testament prophets (Matt. 11:11) because he was able to see the Messiah in the flesh. The way John recognized Jesus was not just by observation but also by direct revelation.

> *"The next day John saw Jesus coming toward him, and said, 'Behold! The Lamb of God who takes away the sin of the world!'"*
>
> JOHN 1:29

John saw the physical Jesus with his natural eyes, but he also saw Jesus' true identity as the Lamb of God in the spirit realm.

While the gifts of the Spirit are for all believers, the three revelation gifts will operate with more frequency in those called to the office of a prophet. John was a prime example of this. It is a combination of the revelation gifts that qualifies a person for the office. Through the discerning of spirits, "John bore witness, saying, 'I saw the Spirit descending from heaven like a dove, and He remained upon Him'" (John 1:32).

John did not see a dove and call it the Spirit. He saw the Spirit *as a dove.* The Holy Spirit certainly is not a common dove, but John discerned Him descending in grace and gentility, like a dove. John was describing in human terms what he saw in the Spirit by the discerning of spirits. This divinely granted insight is so profoundly accurate that to this day the dove is considered a symbol of the Holy Spirit.

Of course, angels are also spirit beings, so the discerning of spirits must include them as well.

Elisha was at total peace when the Syrian army surrounded him in Dothan because unlike his servant, he discerned the angelic spirits surrounding him and knew they far outnumbered their enemies (2 Kings 6:16). We learn quickly in this passage that the way he discerned the angelic host around him was by seeing them; he then prayed that his servant would have his eyes similarly opened. You could say that impartations are not automatic but come by prayer and intention.

When Elisha watched his mentor, Elijah, be caught up into heaven, he saw angelic chariots and horses of fire that came to take the prophet away (2 Kings 2:11). He had to peer into the spirit realm to see that. *The discerning of spirits is a gift that allows seeing/sensing in the spirit about spirits.*

The discerning of spirits is like a spiritual extension to our physical senses.

The spirit realm is invisible but immediately around us. It surrounds and engulfs us, but we cannot experience it with the five physical senses alone. Our natural senses may respond to the spirit realm, but it is only accessible through our spirit man. The discerning of spirits is like a spiritual extension to our physical senses. The gift of discerning of spirits flows through our physical and mental senses to bring us insight from the spiritual plane. Our physical senses are connected to the gift of discerning of spirits because it often causes us to discern through what *seems* to be our physical senses.

Think about how the many prophets in the Bible *heard* the word of the Lord, *saw* angelic beings, sensed good and evil beings, were *touched* by angels, and even *tasted* of the Lord's goodness. This does not mean that only their physical eyes and ears heard and saw into the heavenlies, but rather, that the spiritual realm opened up so that their spirit man could experience its reality.

While not every instance of man's encounter with the spirit realm was a manifestation of the discerning of spirits, they all are examples of the how the spirit realm can be sensed.

Gideon ultimately became a courageous leader, but his start was anything but inspirational. He started out poor and with an inferiority complex, the least of his father's family, hiding from the Midianites to thresh wheat when he had an encounter with an angel. In the natural, Gideon had a lot stacked against him, but the meeting with the angel (Judg. 7:10-15) gave a heavenly boost that was needed for him to accomplish the purposes of God.

THE DISCERNING OF SPIRITS, HEALING, AND DELIVERANCE

"At evening, when the sun had set, they brought to Him all who were sick and those who were

demon-possessed...Then He healed many who were sick with various diseases, and cast out many demons; and He did not allow the demons to speak, because they knew Him."

MARK 1:32,34

One way that the discerning of spirits helps us in ministry is that it enables us to accurately diagnose the source of what oppresses people.

In a way, all sickness has its roots in the devil and demons, but not all sickness is a direct result of demonic activity.

For example, if you maintain an unhealthy diet, your body will respond negatively. It wouldn't be a demon causing the problem, but demons certainly would jump at the opportunity to take advantage of it.

The same is true if you maintain an unhealthy diet of negativity. If you open yourself to too much of the world's news, fear and depression can settle into you. It wouldn't be a demon causing the depression, but again, demons will take advantage of what you hear to bring pictures to your imagination. There is a natural side to sickness because we live in a fallen world with a fallen environment. It would be wrong to say that deliverance from demons is the key to everything, but it would be equally wrong to say that everything has only a natural explanation and that demons are no longer active in the affairs of mankind. There has to be a balance. The gift of discerning of spirits can show us the true source of oppression.

THE LEADINGS OF THE HOLY SPIRIT AND THE GIFT OF DISCERNING OF SPIRITS IN ACTS 16

Acts 16 is a vital chapter for studying the leading of the Spirit. After what the revealed Word of God says, the next immediate way that God leads the believer is with a simple *inward witness*. Since the Holy Spirit is on the inside of us, He leads us from where He is located.

> *"The Spirit Himself bears witness with our spirit...."*
> ROMANS 8:16

The inward witness is your spirit man's sensation of peace—or the lack thereof. Believers must learn to be led by peace. The lack of peace is a sign to go back to the last place you felt it, and then start again from that point.

The lack of peace is a sign to go back to the last place you felt it, and then start again from that point.

After the leading of the inward witness comes the inward voice, which is when your spirit man communicates through your conscious. As a born-again new creation, your conscience is a safe guide because your spirit man is made in the image of God. Our conscience speaks to us in a still, small voice.

"I tell the truth in Christ, I am not lying, my con-science also bearing me witness in the Holy Spirit."

ROMANS 9:1

And lastly—but in a multiplicity of ways—believers are led by the voice of the Holy Spirit. His voice is louder and more authoritative than any other mode of communication.

In Acts 16, we see some major decisions needing to be made—decisions that would impact the move of God in the earth.

"Now when they had gone through Phrygia and the region of Galatia, they were forbidden by the Holy Spirit to preach the word in Asia. After they had come to Mysia, they tried to go into Bithynia, but the Spirit did not permit them. So passing by Mysia, they came down to Troas."

ACTS 16:6-8

It was shocking to me when I first read this. It seemed that Paul and his team did not seek God for their direction, instead traveling the direction they saw fit; they left it to God to say no rather than waiting for His yes. Sometimes, as believers, we make the mistake of refusing to do anything unless we receive a specific word from heaven. Obviously, I am not saying we shouldn't seek God for direction, but there is also a time where, if no specific word comes, we should proceed with what seems best and trust God to tell us otherwise. This is clearly what Paul did in Acts 16.

If no specific word comes, we should proceed with what seems best and trust God to tell us otherwise.

This is not the only way to have God lead us; we should not purposely run ahead of God and make Him play catch up. But there is balance to be had between waiting on God and moving with what seems right if no spiritual red lights are flashing. So, we see here that the voice of the Holy Spirit spoke loud and clear, saving Paul from two consecutive trips that were well intentioned but not the will of God.

Then we see that the word of knowledge was in manifestation when Paul had the vision calling him to Macedonia.

> *"And a vision appeared to Paul in the night. A man of Macedonia stood and pleaded with him, saying, 'Come over to Macedonia and help us.'"*
>
> Acts 16:9

This vision was a result of the cry of the people in Macedonia. God answered their prayers by sending Paul. God has many ways to answer our prayers, even if it means giving someone else a dream or vision to get to us. The move of God in Macedonia was about to be ushered in.

And as if that wasn't spectacular enough, what they encountered in Macedonia was a perfect example of what God was planning to do in the region.

"Now it happened, as we went to prayer, that a certain slave girl possessed with a spirit of divination met us, who brought her masters much profit by fortune-telling. This girl followed Paul and us, and cried out, saying, 'These men are the servants of the Most High God, who proclaim to us the way of salvation.' And this she did for many days.

But Paul, greatly annoyed, turned and said to the spirit, 'I command you in the name of Jesus Christ to come out of her.' And he came out that very hour."

ACTS 16:16-18

In the natural, it would have been tempting for Paul to let this girl on his team. She was favorably known throughout the city, and, theologically, she was *saying all the right things.* In some churches I know, they would have elected her as an elder right away. But something inside Paul was agitated by this woman. He had no peace about her. This went on for a few days, which means Paul sensed something was wrong but did not know what it was or what to do about it.

 The discerning of spirits preserved the purity of the Macedonian call.

Finally, by the discerning of spirits, he recognized that it was not an issue of personality or ability, and Paul turned and *spoke to the spirit.* The discerning of spirits preserved the purity of the Macedonian call.

A RABBIT TRAIL ABOUT THE DISCERNING OF SPIRITS AND THREE LEVELS OF VISIONS

The gift of discerning of spirits can manifest as a spiritual vision, a closed (trance) vision, or an open vision. These three types of visions, in one form or another, can be received when this gift is functioning. Of course, a vision can include more than just a visual experience. As I have said, it is not just our sight that can be touched by the Spirit.

Spiritual Visions

The spiritual vision is the most common and mildest type of vision, but it can carry the highest type of revelation. It is the lowest form because it is more like a flashing mental picture than anything else. We have all experienced this, perhaps during praise and worship at church or maybe in times of prayer when images and unplanned scenarios suddenly pop into our minds.

This form of vision is actually seeing with the inner eyes of the spirit man. It can carry the highest type of revelation because it takes a greater faith to obey a spiritual vision than an open or closed vision; it often seems "normal" when you receive the vision.

Paul received a spiritual vision of Ananias coming to lay hands on him while he was still conscious in the physical realm and aware of his inability to physically see (Acts 9:11-12). This type of vision is usually seen with closed eyes. But with spiritual training and development, a person can receive it with their physical eyes open. The images that come from this type of vision flash before you like they're on a digital screen. They come through your imagination.

Closed Visions

When the gift of discerning of spirits manifests in closed visions, a person receives them in a trance-like state. In this position, the person's physical senses are suspended temporarily, but all the person's spiritual senses are awakened. There is no awareness of what is taking place in the physical realm.

Peter was in a trance when he received a closed vision concerning the acceptance of the "unclean" Gentiles (Acts 10:10-16). It is as if the physical realm is suspended, and the person awakens fully in the spirit realm only.

This experience was so real that when Paul was caught up in a closed vision, he could not tell whether he was in his body or in the spirit (2 Cor. 12:2). In both of these situations, Peter and Paul were so aware of the spiritual realm that they saw it as it really was—more real than the temporary realm of the physical. They were more aware of the spiritual then the natural.

Night visions—or dreams—are another type of closed vision. We have all had dreams that were so real we felt like they were actually happening. This is the experience of a closed vision.

Open Visions

When an open vision manifests, the arena of the spiritual realm is opened to the person whilehe or she is still fully conscious of the physical realm. The physical senses are not suspended; the person sees and senses both the spirit and the physical realm simultaneously. This is a high-level spiritual experience and a foreshadowing of our eternal state.

> This is a high-level spiritual experience and a foreshadowing of our eternal state.

Through an open vision, Zacharias saw an angel of God standing on the right side of the incense altar (Luke 1:11). Peter saw an angel of God that led him out of prison (Acts 12:6-11). They both responded to the spiritual realm and the angels while fully functioning in the natural.

THREE WAYS VISIONS COMMUNICATE

The things that the spirit communicates to us must be properly interpreted. We can find a prime example of this is the Word of God itself.

Hermeneutics, the study of how to interpret the Bible, is a necessary skill to keep our doctrine straight. In fact, we are told to "rightly divide the word" (2 Tim. 2:15). But if the Word can be rightly divided, that means that it can be wrongly divided as well. If the Word of God, communicated to us in our known language, needs dividing—or interpreting—then how much more will the words and images we receive from God through these gifts need interpreting?

Visions are simply vehicles of communication used by our Father. These can be broken down into three main divisions: allegorical visions, message visions, and plain visions.

Allegorical Visions

The first type of vision is an allegorical vision. With this variety of vision, symbols are seen that represent greater truths. While not a vision, Jesus used allegories in teaching with parables. The symbolism of Jesus as the Door, the Good Shepard, or the Bread of Life all needed interpretation. Even the elements of the Lord's Supper, the bread and the wine, have a meaning beyond their natural properties. In an allegorical vision, symbols and signs are used to represent a truth that God wants to relay.

With Daniel, countries were represented by visions of wild beasts and animals (Dan. 7:4-7; 8:4-8).

Peter's vision of unclean animals represented the Gentiles (Acts 10:11-12).

The allegorical vision often requires the most care to interpret.

The interpretation of this type of vision requires both an ear and an eye for the Word and Spirit of God. One of the most basic laws of interpreting this type of vision is that all symbolism must be in line with the Word of God. So, if an image represents something evil in the Bible, any similar image in the allegorical vision must be interpreted accordingly. Since the land of milk and honey is a scriptural symbol of abundance, divine supply, and promises fulfilled, any uses of those images or words received in a vision should be approached from that light. With allegorical visions, not only is a basic Bible knowledge useful, but waiting on God is also vital for correct interpretation.

Message Visions

The second type is when the vision is given to impart a specific message. The key message is not just seen in a picture or image. It is not transmitted as symbolic or allegorical. But it is also not exactly a plain vision since the events will not be played out precisely as they were revealed in the vision.

Paul had this type of message vision when he was waiting in Troas. He saw a Macedonian man calling him to travel over there to help them (Acts 16:9).

We know that Paul knew this vision was not to be interpreted literally because when he and his team arrived in Macedonia, they did not seek out the man that called for Paul in the vision. Instead, Paul's first ministry stop in Macedonia was visiting a group of women (Acts 16:13), and we have no record that he even tried looking for the man in the vision.

 God leads us step by step because all future steps really do not matter if we do not take the immediate one in front of us.

This type of vision really carries only one main message to the recipient. The key message that Paul received from his Macedonian vision was that God wanted him to go to Macedonia; it said nothing of the details to follow. God leads us step by step because all future steps really do not matter if we do not take the immediate one in front of us.

Plain Visions

The third type of vision is what I call a plain vision.

With this type of vision, any people, events, or environments seen and all situations are fulfilled exactly as they were revealed in the vision—right down to the clothing and hair color of the people seen. Plain visions do not need interpretation. They are God showing us a slice of a past, present, or future event. This, of course, means that the word of knowledge and the word of wisdom are involved, but we have already seen that those gifts work together.

Paul had a word of wisdom, but saw it as a plain vision, of Ananias coming in to lay hands on him (Acts 9:12).

Chapter 8

TONGUES AND INTERPRETATION OF TONGUES

"…To another different kinds of tongues, to another the interpretation of tongues."

1 Corinthians 12:10

We are going to look at the gifts of diverse kinds of tongues and the interpretation of tongues together in this chapter. Combined with the gift of prophecy, these gifts are part of the inspirational gifts of utterance. We have seen that any of the gifts can stand alone, but they can also work together. This is truest for these two gifts. Although there are prophetic types and references to diverse tongues and interpretation of tongues in the Old Testament, these two manifestations are reserved only for New Testament believers.

All nine gifts we are looking at can be considered the magnification of a divine seed that is already in us. After all, the giver of these gifts, the Holy Spirit, lives on the inside of us, and when He moved into us, He brought everything He had with Him. Every manifestation of the Holy Spirit is a sudden burst of the Holy Ghost that is already in us.

Every manifestation of the Holy Spirit is a sudden burst of the Holy Ghost that is already in us.

So, while the gift of faith is available for us, we as believers are still to walk by faith in our everyday lives.

Even without the gift of prophecy in operation, we are still to speak words that edify, exhort, and comfort.

Healing is the children's bread and all believers are commanded to lay hands on the sick, but then there are also times where the gifts of healings are made manifest.

So there is no situation in which believers are left lost and hopeless without the gifts; the Holy Spirit inside us provides access to the promises and principles of God's Word. But at the same time, we are told to covet the gifts because they add profit to us. To "add" would imply that we already have something and abundance is being applied. We have the Word. We have the Spirit. And *then* the gifts of the Spirit are added to us!

This is vital to know in studying the gift of diverse tongues. Some believers have either rejected or restricted the place of tongues to their private lives because of a misunderstanding of the role of private and public tongues. Some have thought that all tongues are meant to be private, and so they make no room for this gift to manifest in corporate gatherings. Others have thought that all tongues are for public use only, so they do not place any value in exercising their heavenly prayer language in the secret place.

But as we have seen with the other gifts, there is one aspect of that manifestation that we have on a personal level, and then another that is amplified for the benefit of others. There are tongues for private use and tongues for public demonstration.

Tongues is perhaps the most attacked, reviled, and misunderstood of the spiritual gifts, yet it may be the most powerful.

We need never look to the enemy's tactics to see what God is doing because we have the Holy Spirit as our guide, but it is true that the enemy attacks what he fears the most. Tongues is perhaps the most attacked, reviled, and misunderstood of the spiritual gifts, yet it may be the most powerful.

A Divine Outpouring

"When the Day of Pentecost had fully come, they were all with one accord in one place. And suddenly there came a sound from heaven, as of a rushing mighty wind, and it filled the whole house where they were

*sitting. Then there appeared to them divided tongues,
as of fire, and one sat upon each of them. And they
were all filled with the Holy Spirit and began to speak
with other tongues, as the Spirit gave them utterance."*

ACTS 2:1-4

The upper room outpouring on the day of Pentecost was a spiritual game changer in so many ways. For one thing, it signified to the disciples the completion of Jesus' work—Him sitting down at the right hand of the Father. Jesus had said He would send the Holy Spirit, and this was the sign they were looking for.

It was also the first time the Holy Spirit filled such a large group of people—especially those who, according to the Jewish religious hierarchy, were considered neither priests nor prophets. The Holy Spirit was not just *on* the people as He had been in the Old Testament, but He was now *in* them!

You can easily see the significance of this event. It would be easy to assume the Holy Spirit would want to show Himself in a significant way. It always fascinates me that the Holy Spirit did not take over the disciples' hands to make them start laying hands on the multitudes. He did not take over their legs to cause them to run far and wide declaring the gospel. He did not take over their minds so they would immediately have the thoughts of God. He did not take over their ears so they could hear His voice audibly. The Holy Spirit merely empowered their vocal cords, and they spoke a new language. Apparently, the Holy Spirit valued their tongues and the language they produced more than the other parts of their bodies.

Later on, James, who was present in the upper room, would say, "...If anyone does not stumble in word, he is a perfect man, able also to bridle the whole body. Indeed, we put bits in horses' mouths that they may obey us, and we turn their whole body. Look also at ships: although they are so large and are driven by fierce winds, they are turned by a very small rudder wherever the pilot desires. Even so the tongue is a little member and boasts great things... But no man can tame the tongue. It is an unruly evil, full of deadly poison" (James 3:2-4,8).

James understood that the tongue was the rudder of a person's life. No man armed with any philosophical or religious code had been able to tame the tongue, which, in turn, was the rudder of his life. But on the day of Pentecost, the Holy Spirit took over and empowered the disciples' tongues with a heavenly language that could steer their lives in a heavenly direction.

PAUL'S KEY TO REVELATION

Because of the upper room outpouring and Paul's declaration to the Corinthians, we know that all the writers of the New Testament spoke in tongues. Paul, of course, is unique among New Testament authors because in the natural, he had no direct encounter with Jesus. All of Paul's experiences with Jesus were post resurrection. They were all spiritual encounters. We also know that Paul proudly declared, "I thank my God I speak with tongues more than you all" (1 Cor. 14:18). So it is evident that Paul had an active prayer life with tongues. But we know this was not the public demonstration of the gift. In the very next verse, Paul says, "...Yet in the church I would rather speak five words with my understanding, that I may teach others also, than ten thousand words in a tongue" (1 Cor. 14:19).

We see clearly that when Paul referenced speaking in tongues more than the Corinthians, he meant in private. Paul spoke in tongues aggressively!

> *"For he who speaks in a tongue does not speak to men but to God, for no one understands him; however, in the spirit he speaks mysteries."*
>
> 1 CORINTHIANS 14:2

The Pauline revelation contained in the epistles forms the backbone of New Testament theology. The revelation of what happened "behind the scenes" of the cross and in the working of our redemption is only revealed in the Epistles. The working of God from the cross to the throne is only found in the Epistles. The position of the believer seated in heavenly places in Christ is only found in the Epistles. The believer's position of victory over the enemy is only found in the Epistles. And the bulk of these truths are found in Paul's writings. Clearly, all sixty-six books of the Bible are God-breathed, inspired by the Spirit, and of equal value, but it would be fair to ask how Paul came across such a wealth of revelation.

Paul's writings are so packed with deep truth that even Peter admitted "...as also in all [Paul's] epistles, speaking in them of these things, in which are some things *hard to understand*, which untaught and unstable people twist to their own destruction, as they do also *the rest of the Scriptures*" (2 Pet. 3:16).

Paul's writings were so profound that even Peter admitted some portions were hard to understand. We can only conclude that part of the reason these deep revelations came to Paul was because he had prayed and spoken out the mysteries of God as he prayed and spoke in tongues.

Through tongues and interpretation, the Spirit once said to me, "Utterance always comes before manifestations."

The manifestation of Paul's epistles were the result of the utterance he first had in the Spirit. Of course, all the other New Testament authors also spoke in tongues, so the same principle applies to them.

We can only conclude that part of the reason these deep revelations came to Paul was because he had prayed and spoken out the mysteries of God as he prayed and spoke in tongues.

How deep was Paul's revelation in the Epistles? Peter compared it to "the rest of the Scriptures." This means that within the first generation of believers, they were already recognizing that Paul's writings were Scripture—God-breathed! Such is the depth of speaking out the mysteries of the Spirit.

DIVERSE KINDS OF TONGUES

This gift of diverse kinds of tongues can be simply understood this way: It is a supernatural utterance from the Holy Spirit in languages never learned by the speaker and rarely comprehended by the hearers.

Diverse kinds of tongues have nothing to do with the linguistic ability, mind, or intellect of the believer the gift flows through. It is a dramatic outward manifestation of the mind of the Spirit flowing through the believer's speech faculties. When an individual is speaking with tongues, his or her mind, intellect, and understanding are not involved; this is a spiritual operation that the soul is not involved in. It originates from the flow of God's Spirit. The believer's will is active in that he or she must consciously yield to the prompting of the Spirit. In yielding the will, the believer then yields his or her spirit, vocal cords, and physical tongue to the Spirit. But the mind, the Spirit that is operating the message itself, is the mind of God through the Holy Spirit.

In the same way that it was not Paul's medical training that caused him to minister healing when Publius' father had a fever (Acts 28:7-8), messages given through the gift of tongues have nothing to do with the believer's language ability. The gift of diverse tongues is a verbal, vocal manifestation. It is not an intellectual, linguistic miracle.

After I became born again, leaving behind my Catholic background, I became curious about the charismatic, Spirit-filled church I joined. The whole scene of clapping, lifting hands during worship, and witnessing miracles in church was foreign to me. But the thing that caught my attention immediately was that funny language charismatics spoke in. I didn't know until later that it even had a term attached to it. I had never even heard of "tongues."

One evening, after a particularly stirring service, I went home thinking that if this tongues thing was real, I wanted it. That night I had a vivid dream. I was in a worship service, and there were people everywhere with their hands lifted. They were all speaking and worshiping in tongues. In my dream, I heard the worship leader encourage everyone else to lift their hands and join in the worship. I did and found myself speaking fluently in tongues. This carried on for what seemed like a while, then I woke up to find that I was still speaking in tongues in my bed!

We will look at the role of tongues in the everyday life of a believer later on, but it is important to know that there is a difference between our private prayer language—like we have seen in the life of Paul—and the public message-delivering manifestation of tongues, which, for the benefit of the hearers, must always be accompanied by an equally Spirit-inspired interpretation in a known language.

Paul designates this as the gift of diverse kinds of tongues (1 Cor. 12:10). There is a vast difference between the gift of diverse kinds of tongues and the basic gift of the believer praying in tongues. The gift of diverse kinds of tongues is a supernatural utterance given by God through believers in an unknown, previously unlearned language. Since it is in an unknown tongue, it needs to be interpreted through the twin gift of the interpretation of tongues for the edification of others. Together, the gift of diverse tongues and the interpretation of those tongues equals the simple gift of prophecy, bringing a message of edification, exhortation, and comfort.

The gift of tongues is a message through a believer from the Spirit of God to men, while prayer in tongues is an utterance by men—empowered by the Holy Spirit—to God. The directional flow of these utterances is in the opposite direction. One comes downward from God. The other goes upwards to God.

The gift of tongues is a message through a believer from the Spirit of God to men, while prayer in tongues is an utterance by men—empowered by the Holy Spirit—to God.

God understands all languages, both of men and angels, so there is no need for any interpretation in our prayers to Him in tongues. But this is not the case when it is a downward message in tongues from God to us; we need an interpretation since we do not understand all languages of man, much less of angels. When Paul rightly instructed the church in Corinth to have an interpretation of tongues in their meetings, he was referring to the vocal gift of tongues, not the believer's prayer in tongues (1 Cor. 14:5,27-28).

However, I have found that since there can be an interpretation for public tongues, there can also be, at a certain depth of praying in tongues, an interpretation for utterances in our private prayer language. *Praying in the spirit is not just praying in tongues; it is praying from the location of the spirit.* From there, believers might pray in tongues or just their known language.

There will often be a switch between tongues and the known language. It would help your prayer that when this happens, you do not pause to consider what the English words mean or imply, but just continue praying in tongues until another word in English comes out. Speak that word when it comes to you and then go back to tongues. The reason for this is because since you are praying from the location of the spirit, you do not want your head getting in the way of what is going on.

When I lead prayer meetings, I always instruct the people that as we are praying, if the words "Aunt Susie" come out, then just say that and go right back to tongues. Don't stop and try to figure out what is wrong with Aunt Susie, or worse, try to add into your prayer what you think is wrong with Aunt Susie. That will get you out of the Spirit and straight into praying from the flesh.

We can pray for the Spirit to enlarge our ability to interpret our tongues. Obviously, God would not require us to understand everything we pray in tongues because there is an element of praying out His mysteries when we do. This is a preventative measure because it keeps the devil from knowing what we are praying.

As we develop our sensitivity to the things of the Spirit, we can receive a basic understanding of what we had been praying about. This spiritual sensitivity can be matured by nurturing and spiritual development. Developing your spirit man through prayer, meditation, and studying God's word matures your spirit and its sensitivity to the anointing within. Yielding to the gift of the interpretation of tongues is a development of learning to cooperate with the anointing.

The anointing within a believer is for their successful running of the race God has set for his or her life. The anointing upon a believer is for the successful serving of others by the delivering of God's grace and power.

Another way to edify ourselves is by singing in the spirit and singing interpretations. This would fall somewhere under the category of psalms, hymns, and spiritual songs. I am not musical in that I do not play any instruments, nor have I ever led the singing part of a service. So I tend to lean toward speaking in tongues more than singing in tongues. When I enter that flow, rather than sing out the inspired utterances, I speak them out.

Paul said that when the public gift of tongues is in manifestation, an interpretation must be rendered after every three messages (1 Cor. 14:27). This has been interpreted to mean that there must be no more than three messages of tongues at any given meeting. But if we look closely at these verses, we see that Paul was not referring to a limit of three messages per meeting, he was simply emphasizing the need to balance the messages in tongues with appropriate interpretations. Paul cautioned against allowing too many messages in tongues to be released *without interpretation*; it would go against the principle purpose of spiritual gifts, which is for the profit of the Body.

The gift of diverse or various kinds of tongues is a vocal sign gift designed by the Spirit for public ministry. This manifestation is unique to this Church age that we are a part of; it was part of the divine announcement of the Church's birth on the day of Pentecost and has accompanied the Church ever since. There have been times in Church history where it seemed like this manifestation, both in private and in public, was all but snuffed out, just as there have been times where it seemed like the Word and the Spirit's movement had been snuffed out. But God always has a remnant.

With the turn of the twentieth century, there was a fresh outpouring of the Spirit that reverberated through the Church world so that now the Spirit-filled experience is considered the norm in most church circles. A new expectation for signs, wonders, and the voice of the Holy Spirit swept the Church into a new realm of the supernatural. In answer to this hunger, the gifts of the Spirit made their way to the forefront of the Church world again.

A new expectation for signs, wonders, and the voice of the Holy Spirit swept the Church into a new realm of the super-natural.

As with all the other gifts of the Spirit, the gift of diverse or different kinds of tongues is not the ability to learn quickly and then speak and communicate in various languages. It is not part of what missionaries have done for years in foreign lands to reach the unreached.

Practically speaking, those who would move in this gift would have to first be Spirit filled, Spirit baptized, and speak in tongues in their private lives—or at least be open to that manifestation. It would seem that tongues in the life of a believer are the door to other manifestations. Of course, the gifts can manifest in any believer, but tongues in our private prayer lives keeps us aware of the Spirit's presence.

> *"How is it then, brethren? Whenever you come together, each of you has a psalm, has a teaching, has a tongue, has a revelation, has an interpretation. Let all things be done for edification."*
> 1 CORINTHIANS 14:26

This manifestation of the Spirit is a part of congregational life. It has the same place in a church meeting as teaching or sharing a revelation. Together with interpretation of tongues, these two manifestations equal the simple gift of prophecy. Like prophecy, they minister edification, exhortation, and comfort to those in attendance.

> *"Therefore tongues are for a sign, not to those who believe but to unbelievers; but prophesying is not for unbelievers but for those who believe. Therefore if the whole church comes together in one place, and all speak with tongues, and there come in those who are uninformed or unbelievers, will they not say that you are out of your mind?"*
> 1 CORINTHIANS 14:22-23

Due to there being such an abundance of public tongues in manifestation when the Corinthian church gathered, Paul cautioned that tongues, if they were not interpreted, would have a reverse effect. Those that were not believers would see the tongues as madness instead of divine utterance since no understanding would come without an interpretation. Of course, for those that were not believers, they had no spiritual sense of the move of the Spirit and could only depend on their physical senses to determine what was happening at the meeting. So, to cater to that need, an interpretation was mandatory. With all this, it's important to see that at no time did Paul prohibit tongues, but rather, sought to provide guidelines on how they should be exercised.

> *"Though I speak with the tongues of men and of angels...."*
>
> 1 CORINTHIANS 13:1

Diverse tongues, from God's perspective, include tongues of men and of angels.

I have had people tell me that all tongues in the Bible were actual spoken languages that were not known by those speaking when the gift manifested and that modern-day tongues are just gibberish. What Paul said here disproves that. Think about this: if unbelievers attended a meeting and heard the believers speaking in a foreign language they had not learned, those who did not believe would not say they were "out of their minds" for speaking a foreign language. They may not have understood it, but it did not make those who did "out of their minds." I have been to many foreign lands and as I've told you, I am monolingual, so there are many tongues that I do not understand. But I have never said to myself when I heard them speaking, *They must be out of their minds.*

I have witnessed situations where the gift of diverse tongues was in operation and the tongue that manifested was in a known tongue.

Many upscale consumer products we use are made in third world countries—quite a few of those in factories throughout Southeast Asia. Oftentimes dormitories will be built around these factories to house the workers. There was a time where my team and I were allowed into those dormitories in one nation to have meetings and minister to the people living there. After I had ministered the Word and given an opportunity for the people to respond, we were praising the Lord and laying hands on people to be filled with the Holy Spirit. I came to one young lady who had tears streaming from her closed eyes. Her hands were raised, and I heard her fluently praising God in English. She was using phrases like, "Glory to His name." "Praise the glorious name." And even, "Worthy is the Lamb of God."

I thought this young lady was one of the few believers working at the factory, and so I moved away thinking how rare it was to find someone who not only spoke English but was fluent enough to be praising God in our tongue. I motioned for the other team members to quietly pass by her and listen to her praising God. She was the first fluent English speaker we came across that whole week. It was glorious!

We lingered in the dormitory after the meeting to fellowship with the people living there. I asked the supervisor—who was a believer and had helped us get into the factories—about the woman praising in English; I thought she would be a good interpreter for our future visits. The supervisor looked at me blankly and said the woman in question was a new believer who definitely did not speak or understand English. I insisted she did, and he finally called her over so I could see for myself. He was right. She did not speak even a word of English!

> *"For they heard them speak with tongues and magnify God."*
>
> ACTS 10:46

There have also been times while ministering that I have entered a place in the Spirit where it seemed like tongues were my natural language. There have been many an occasion where this has happened and it made speaking in English a challenge because I was so aware of the spirit realm. One time, I was actually caught up into the Spirit like this for over six hours and could hardly communicate in English. It was like being swept into a trance that only affected my speech.

There have also been occasions where this has happened and other ministers attending the meetings would be caught up in the Spirit with me. When this happens, we can actually converse in tongues and respond to each other with a "knowing" in our spirits. There is a level of spirit-to-spirit communication that is available to believers in the same way that we connect with others over a shared interest.

WHEN I FELT PROMPTED TO ASK FOR MORE

As long as I've been in ministry, I have had an ease with laying hands on the sick. By that I mean that I would regularly have inner promptings to minister to the sick by the laying on of hands. As time progressed, and I learned to cooperate with the anointing more, I found that the laying on of hands was not the only way that I could minister healing. Many times I could also sense an "unease" in areas of my body that corresponded to areas in the bodies of others in the services that needed healing. I would call these out, describe them, and healings would spontaneously occur. These were words of knowledge leading to the gifts of healings.

There was once a season where I was stirred to press for more of the manifestations in my life. We are instructed to "covet earnestly the best gifts" (1 Cor. 12:31). This does not just mean one of the best of the nine gifts (which would be the one that is most needed in any situation) but also the best of the diverse manifestations of each of the gifts.

> There was once a season where I was stirred to press for more of the manifestations in my life. We are instructed to "covet earnestly the best gifts" (1 Cor. 12:31).

I started saying to God, "Father, if You can tell me what sickness needs healing in a room by causing warmth or tightness in parts of my body, why can't I ask for even more specificity?"

I have found that God is the source of all inspired prayer. He inspires us to pray specific prayers because He desires us to have what He inspires us to pray for.

A few months after praying that way, I was in the middle of a weeklong series of meetings in a midwestern church. Many inspired utterances and supernatural occurrences had already happened that week, but as I moved to close the service one particular night, I paced in the front of the church waiting to see if there was anything else the Holy Spirit wanted before we dismissed. I was quietly speaking in tongues as the congregation spontaneously worshipped and prayed.

Suddenly, the flow of tongues changed and became more authoritative. I realized that I had shifted from praying in tongues to giving a public tongue that required an interpretation. I quickly quieted myself and immediately the words bubbled out.

"Joshua James[3]! Joshua James! Joshua James!"

This happened three times and then I fell quiet. I sensed another flow of tongues and this time the interpretation was, "Raise up! Raise up! It's not over! Don't say you won't!"

"Raise up! Raise up! It's not over! Don't say you won't!"

Strangely, after that I sensed the unction lift and no other utterance came. The congregation looked at me expectantly, but there was nothing else for me to say. I have learned that we

3 Names have been changed.

must not try to prolong a service past the flow of the anointing. We must end meetings when the anointing lifts.

I had the worship leader lead a song, and then I made my way to the pastor's office upstairs. I usually try to stay down front after services to meet with people, but I had been advised to leave immediately because of the size of the crowd that night.

About ten minutes after I entered the pastor's office, the service closed and one of the associate pastors came running into the room. He excitedly told me that a young man had come sobbing to the front of the church, where the leaders were standing, asking if I had really called out the name "Joshua James." When he was told that I had, he shared with them that six months ago he and his wife had lost a child in the womb. They had wanted to name their son *Joshua James*, but when they lost him, they had been so badly affected by the death that they had said they would never try for another baby. Not only had the calling out of their son's name caught their attention, the exhortation of, "Raise up. It's not over. Don't say you won't" corrected their decision not to try for more children. Two years later when I was back in the same church, I was pleasantly surprised to see the couple after the service...with a newborn son!

Although that was a public demonstration of the gift of tongues and interpretation of tongues, it was really a private message for that couple. I regularly see this manifestation operate that way.

At another church, as I laid hands on people and ministered as the Spirit led, I felt drawn to an older couple seated at the back of the auditorium. They were seated by themselves on the last row and had not really participated in the service. The reason I sometimes walk around rather than calling individuals out to pray for them is that in many of those situations, I want the congregation to keep their focus on the Spirit, not on what I am doing. I especially do this if the auditorium is large enough for me to walk around comfortably or if the congregation is new to my teaching. The churches that have had me minister before are usually accustomed to how I operate.

My heart was drawn to the old couple at the back, and so I made my way over to them. It was almost too far to walk, but as I got closer, they looked like if I had called them forward, they'd have bolted for the door instead.

When I came to them and reached out my hands to them, a bubbling of tongues came gushing out of me followed by the interpretation.

"You are not done here. You are not done here. I have planted you here, and I still have things for you here." They both looked uncertain as the Lord ministered to them through the word.

After the service, the pastors told me that they had been an integral part of the church for years, but about a year ago, they had visited another church when it had a guest speaker and then decided to stay there. The past six months, they had started sporadically attending the midweek service, but they seemed uncertain how to move forward. But that night, the Lord gave them a clear answer.

INTERPRETATION OF TONGUES

Just as God moves supernaturally to empower a believer's linguistic abilities through the gift of diverse tongues, God then completes that miraculous message with the interpretation into a known language for the benefit of those in attendance.

This manifestation of the interpretation of tongues is a supernatural interpretation of a message in tongues delivered to the Church. The message in tongues is then made understandable through this gift. Of course, this is the gift of *interpretation* of tongues *not* the gift of *translation* of tongues. So it's possible to have a long message in tongues and a short interpretation or a short message and a longer interpretation. You could have two people with the gift of interpretation interpreting the same message in tongues, and they both wouldn't use the same words or expressions. But regardless, the basic essence of the message God intended would be delivered through the manifestation.

If the believer delivering the interpretation tried to match the length of the interpretation with the length of the message in tongues, that would be leaning on the natural to move into the supernatural. That is not how any of the gifts work. They are all supernaturally inspired and not gauged by the natural world.

Tongues, both private and public, bypass the mind, but the interpretation flows from God through the mind of man. I don't mean that the believer has anything to do with the message itself, but the believer has *everything* to do with expressing that message. That believer's upbringing and his command of language are both factors in how the message will be delivered. In the natural, I have worked with many interpreters while ministering around the world, and I have seen this in action with natural messages.

Tongues, both private and public, bypass the mind, but the interpretation flows from God through the mind of man.

When I first started preaching using interpreters, I was always surprised that the length of what they said did not always correspond with the length of what I said. I used to wonder if they were actually preaching their own message.

It seems to me that the most common way that an interpretation is received is when after a message in tongues is given, there is a sense of gentle pressure, a bubbling up, almost a knowing, usually followed by a word, phrase, or scripture with an interpretation. If the individual will step out and act on this inner leading, the rest of the message will come.

The interpretation could also be initially received as a series of thoughts or even mental pictures, then the believer receiving them describes what he sees. Frequently, I will hear words in English that I then repeat aloud.

It is less frequent, but I have witnessed situations where a message in tongues was given in a foreign language unknown by the one giving the message, but it is recognizable by someone else in the meeting that speaks that language. Obviously, that is not an interpretation of tongues since the hearer actually understood the message in the natural; however, the accuracy of the one delivering the message in the unlearned tongue, then verified by a fluent speaker, testifies to the divine beauty of these gifts.

Those who flow in the gift of diverse tongues have a scriptural prompting in First Corinthians 14:13 to also ask for the accompanying ability to interpret those tongues; God's purpose through this manifestation, as is the case with all the gifts, is for the edification and building up of the Church. God intends to be heard.

I have seen that the interpretation of tongues can come through inspirationally speaking the message as it comes, or it can come as a vision the believer then describes. To do either requires a measure of faith, so just as we saw that prophecy is proportionate to our faith (Rom. 12:6), so also tongues and the interpretation of tongues come in proportion to our faith. After all, the message through the twin gifts of tongues and interpretation equals that of a prophecy.

Chapter Nine

THE RIVER OF THE SPIRIT

"He who believes in Me, as the Scripture has said, out of his heart will flow rivers of living water.' But this He spoke concerning the Spirit, whom those believing in Him would receive; for the Holy Spirit was not yet given, because Jesus was not yet glorified."

—John 7:38-39

The real gift we received when we became born again is not nine separate gifts but rather the single gift of the Holy Spirit Himself. All these *rivers* flow from this one gift.

When we have used the word *gift* both in the Bible and in this study, we have not meant it as it's understood today—a present that the receiver has full control of without further involvement from the giver. In the context of First Corinthians 12, the word *gift* is used to imply that these manifestations do not originate from us but from an independent source that resides in us. So these *gifts* are simply *manifestations* that originate separately from us, but by divine decree, flow as a gift through us.

This distinction is vital to see because it takes us from thinking that we only have access to one or two manifestations to seeing that we have the Giver of the gifts on the inside of us. When the river flowed into us, every drop, every puddle, every pool, and every stream contained in it flowed into us as well! And since it is all in us, it can now flow from us.

FREE GIFTS

Prophecy and Tongues

> *"Pursue love, and desire spiritual gifts, but especially that you may prophesy."*
> 1 CORINTHIANS 14:1

> *"Therefore let him who speaks in a tongue pray that he may interpret."*
> 1 CORINTHIANS 14:13

> *"Therefore, brethren, desire earnestly to prophesy, and do not forbid to speak with tongues."*
> 1 CORINTHIANS 14:39

In these passages, Paul makes it clear that we are encouraged and expected to take up a more purposeful attitude in the manifestations of the Spirit in our lives. Clearly, we are to do more than passively wait for the "stirring of the waters" or for some moving of the Spirit while our faith is disengaged. We are scripturally justified in seeking, expecting, and hungering for these manifestations.

We are scripturally justified in seeking, expecting, and hungering for these manifestations.

As we've said, the word *gift* does not occur in the original versions of First Corinthians 12:1 and 14:1. These verses simply speak of *spirituals*; they are referring to elements in the worship and activity of a local church setting that originate in the spiritual realm. Clearly, *spirituals* covers a wide variety of manifestations and should not to be restricted to the nine manifestations mentioned in First Corinthians 12:8-10.

The translators, however, have correctly added the word *gifts* because the context of the chapter makes it plain that this is Paul's true intention in these passages.

Also, the word *gifts* (*charismata*) is actually used in First Corinthians 12:4, 9, and 31. So calling these manifestations *spiritual gifts* would be appropriate.

Gift comes from the same Greek root as *grace—charis*. In Romans 6:23, Paul uses the same word speaking of our salvation: "*Gift* of eternal life." To think we can earn these nine manifestations or any of God's gifts would be as foolish as thinking that we could merit salvation by works.

Putting any of the gifts before the giver would be a mistake. To be gift conscious over being giver conscious would be a mistake. But it would be equally a mistake to be conscious of

God and ignore the gifts He intends for us. He is a "rewarder of those that diligently seek Him" (Heb. 11:6).

Either position would be a ditch to avoid.

Any gift, especially from the Father, ought to be given from the motivation of love, not manipulation. If we get the mistaken interpretation that the gifts of the Spirit work in us in a mechanical sense, then we have totally misunderstood the Father's heart. He does not give us gifts to use us, but rather, to bless and increase us. Many times I hear people talk or pray about how they want God to "use them." I understand that they desire God to move through them and I appreciate their sincerity, but I've always been a little cautious with that verbiage. Our Father doesn't ever "use" us as if we were some garden tool to be tossed aside when the gardening is done. But God does seek to express Himself through us. That is what these manifestations are. They are expressions and manifestations of the Father's heart.

But God does seek to express Himself through us. That is what these manifestations are. They are expressions and manifestations of the Father's heart.

Gifts must be given and received from the heart. To legalize it any other way would be to go against the spirit of gift giving and carry it over to wage earning! Paul was not writing to the Corinthians about spiritual wages but spiritual gifts!

As God's sons and daughters, we are never expected to be mere "spirit mediums," an empty shell possessed by a wandering spirit. We are to be living vessels in a vibrant relationship with our Father. We are not to be robots for the Master's use. We are to be sons and daughters representing our Father!

It is not on us to earn the gifts, but it is on us to grow toward maturity through fellowship with and yieldedness to the Father. We do this by cultivating a relationship with Him through the Word and the Spirit. And it is always in that order: Word and then Spirit, never the other way around. If you do not know the Word, how will you recognize what the Spirit is saying to you?

A believer's relationship with the Word determines his or her relationship with the Father, which determines the believer's faith level, and his or her faith level can determine his or her fluency in the gifts.

Spirit-led prayer is the womb of learning the art of yielding to God. Yielding to God is vital for any of the gifts to manifest. Not knowing about the gifts will leave them unwrapped, and thus, unused.

Spirit-led prayer is the womb of learning the art of yielding to God. Not knowing about the gifts will leave them unwrapped, and thus, unused.

So there are issues that cause the gifts not to manifest, but all are easily remedied.

While we cannot earn these gifts, we are responsible for cultivating an environment where they can flourish. The principles of faith, yielding to the unction of the Spirit, and setting our desires toward these manifestations are all ways we make room for the gifts to flow.

The giving and exercise of spiritual gifts have some definite purposes. These manifestations are always to glorify God by edifying the Church. These manifestations must always be administered in an attitude of love. Since God Himself is love, all His gifts come from the place of love as well. We could say that *if it is not love, it is not God.*

One way we can look at the timeline of the Bible is that the Old Testament was the dispensation of Jehovah God, the Gospels were the dispensation of Jesus, and from the book of Acts on, the dispensation of the Holy Spirit.

All three members of the Godhead were actively present throughout the biblical record, but there seems to a rotation of prominence.

In this Church age, we are in the season of the Spirit.

With the Holy Spirit in prominence, these gifts that the Holy Spirit bestows on the Church have the potential to be in full manifestation. The greater works of Jesus are now a reality because of the sheer magnitude of believers worldwide who have the same access to the anointing and gifts that flowed through His ministry.

The manifestation of the Holy Spirit is given to each one for the profit of all. Every believer has *already* received something from the Holy Spirit that they can bring to build up of the whole Body of Christ. No single believer is left gift-less by the Holy Spirit. Our Father does not overlook any of His children.

> No single believer is left gift-less by the Holy Spirit. Our Father does not overlook any of His children.

As we give ourselves to understanding what the gifts of the Holy Spirit are and how they operate, we are better poised to flow with the manifestations of the Holy Spirit. The gifts of the Holy Spirit should be encouraged and cultivated to operate in an orderly manner every time believers come together. There is a time and place for each of these gifts to manifest because there will always be needs represented when believers gather. These manifestations are the Spirit's answer.

The Spirit's anointings for revelation gifts, power gifts, and vocal gifts all operate differently. We can continually cultivate and maintain sensitivity to which type of anointing is in manifestation so that we can allow for the right gift to operate at the right time.

TUNING TO THE BANDWIDTH OF THE SPIRIT

Of the rivers of the Spirit that started flowing once the Spirit was given to dwell in us, the one that we can most readily step into is the river of tongues. Of course, I am not talking about the manifestation of public tongues that requires the twin manifestation of the interpretation of tongues, but the Spirit-empowered prayer language that began on the day of Pentecost. This particular manifestation opened the disciples for all the other manifestations to flow through them. In fact, after Acts 2, we see the manifestations continually in every chapter to follow in the book of Acts.

Paul would later explain in his epistle to the Corinthians that "…He who speaks in a tongue edifies himself" (1 Cor. 14:4). It takes divine edification to have divine manifestation.

Praying in tongues is a simple way to sensitize and tune your spirit to the leadings of the Holy Spirit. It gets your spirit on the frequency of the Holy Spirit's bandwidth. It's the primer to all the other manifestations because it puts your spirit man on the same page as the Holy Spirit. The Spirit is always wanting to bring profit to all, and the way He does that is always through one of the manifestations of the Spirit.

> Praying in tongues is a simple way to sensitize and tune your spirit to the leadings of the Holy Spirit. It gets your spirit on the frequency of the Holy Spirit's bandwidth.

Take time to develop your spirit self by speaking in tongues throughout your day. I am continually amazed by what divine insight and direction comes up as I do. It can come up as a thought or an inner image. I would say that the majority of times when I have moved into the manifestations of the Spirit, they have come by the quiet leading of the Spirit that comes by taking time to pray and speak in tongues through the day.

BOLDLY MANIFEST

"Now, Lord, look on their threats, and grant to Your servants that with all boldness they may speak Your word, by stretching out Your hand to heal, and that signs and wonders may be done through the name of Your holy Servant Jesus."

ACTS 4:29-30

Regardless of how clearly the Spirit speaks to you or shows you things, there will come a moment where you have to decide if you will step out and risk being utterly wrong, or in the case of the early disciples, being right and facing angry mobs. Either way, it will take boldness to step out into the manifestations of the Spirit. Actually, I would rather someone be reverent to the point of being a little cautious when moving in the gifts, as opposed to someone who is convinced they cannot be wrong.

Obviously, I am not suggesting that we be timid or fearful about the manifestations, but that being over confident also leaves God out. I have seen self-absorbed people who were convinced that they had God leading them despite the counsel of spiritually mature, qualified leaders and the clear interpretation of Scripture. They usually have to twist scriptures to suit their personal revelations. If you listen to some of these people that always seem to have Jesus tell them nearly everything every day, it would appear that the Holy Spirit exists only to confirm what they already wanted to do.

True boldness is a choice to be obedient. This means it is likely something that on your own you would either have not thought to do or rather not done. Even if you were occasionally wrong, as anyone who is moving in the gifts will testify that they have been, you need not fear the wrath of God over your mistake. Our Father is not wrathful, and if your pure motivation was to be an extension of the Hand of God, why wouldn't His grace and mercy cover and redeem you in that situation?

True boldness is a choice to be obedient.

The early Church understood and prayed this way because boldness was the key to the preaching of the gospel and the subsequent healings, signs, and wonders. Since boldness was needed to do the speaking and proclaiming of the gospel, we can see that boldness was needed for the manifestations that followed.

Boldness is the fruit of obedience. Obedience doesn't mean God drags you by the hair, kicking and screaming into submission. Obedience is a simple gesture of yieldedness. Yielding is easy when you know that the one you are yielding to is good and trustworthy. Getting to know the Spirit through the

Word and prayer will bring us to a place of increasing boldness to step out in the manifestations.

THE MOTIVATION OF LOVE

"Though I speak with the tongues of men and of angels, but have not love, I have become sounding brass or a clanging cymbal. And though I have the gift of prophecy, and understand all mysteries and all knowledge, and though I have all faith, so that I could remove mountains, but have not love, I am nothing. And though I bestow all my goods to feed the poor, and though I give my body to be burned, but have not love, it profits me nothing."

1 CORINTHIANS 13: 1-4

The spiritual manifestations of First Corinthians 12 are all heavenly interruptions of divine love into the natural world!

Love is the reason the manifestations are made available from God, and love is the means by which they are meant to be administered.

It is not by accident that between the catalog of manifestations in First Corinthians 12 and the description of their use in First Corinthians 14, is an entire chapter of love in First Corinthians 13. Love is the reason the manifestations are made available from God, and love is the means by which they are meant to be administered. Since faith works by love and all we do as believers is to be done in faith, it makes scriptural sense that these manifestations are to be expressions of loves as well.

The gifts of the Spirit are not meant to be used to embarrass others, "one up" each other, or to posture yourself above another. The gifts are for the profit of all but never at the expense of others.

I have seen situations where people tried to "out prophesy" each other to see who could deliver the more spectacular prophecy or use supposed words of knowledge and wisdom to embarrass and expose people publicly without discretion. I've also seen where an excessively dramatic show has been made when ministering to the sick, drawing more attention to the one ministering than to the Healer Himself.

The fact that these spiritual manifestations can be abused is clearly seen in the Corinthian church itself; this was partly why Paul wrote the first and second Corinthian epistles, to correct but not restrict their usage. What is the answer to the proper use of these gifts? Use them from and for the love of God and others!

ABOUT DR. JAMES TAN

Dr. James Tan is a visionary leader who declares the goodness of God to a new generation of believers. Called to raise the standard of the Word and the Spirit, he ministers scriptural insights and demonstrations of the Holy Spirit to bless and empower believers internationally, cross-culturally, and beyond denominational lines.

Dr. James Tan advises and oversees a growing number of churches and ministries. In addition to planting and building churches, he also coordinates humanitarian outreaches in third-world nations.

Let's stay connected!

Facebook
I Am Just James@justdrjames

Instagram
I Am Just James@justdrjames

The Harrison House Vision

Proclaiming the truth and the power

of the Gospel of Jesus Christ with excellence.

Challenging Christians

to live victoriously,

grow spiritually,

know God intimately.

Connect with us on
f Facebook @ **HarrisonHousePublishers**
and **◎** Instagram @ **HarrisonHousePublishing**
so you can stay up to date with news
about our books and our authors.

Visit us at **www.harrisonhouse.com**
for a complete product listing as well as
monthly specials for wholesale distribution.